Fiachra Ó Ceallaigh, ofm.
28/1/74 .

ó phádraig Ó Fearaíle.

Fiachra Ó Ceallaigh, ofm.
Rinn Mhic Ghormáin

Student Counselling in Practice

Student Counselling in Practice

Audrey Newsome, Brian J. Thorne,
Keith L. Wyld

Appointments and Counselling Service, University of Keele

 UNIVERSITY OF LONDON PRESS LTD

ISBN O 340 16772 6 Boards
ISBN O 340 17796 9 Unibook

University of London Press Ltd
St Paul's House, Warwick Lane, London EC4P 4AH

Printed in Great Britain by
T. & A. Constable Ltd, Edinburgh

Acknowledgments

Our debt to those who have either trained or influenced us in other ways is enormous. They will hear their own words in our text and if we had had the time to be scholarly they would have featured in countless references and footnotes. Without them we would not be the people we are and this book would never have been written.

A particular debt of gratitude is owed to Dr H. M. Taylor, formerly Vice-Chancellor of Keele, whose support and encouragement enabled the Counselling Service to come into being; to Professor W. A. C. Stewart, the present Vice-Chancellor, for his unfailing interest in the continued development of our work and to two distinguished friends and teachers from America, Professor D. E. Super and Professor C. G. Wrenn.

'Resolve to be thyself: and know, that he
Who finds himself, loses his misery.'

Matthew Arnold

Contents

Preface

A few years ago counselling was a word which fell strangely on British ears: if it meant anything at all it tended to be associated with the Marriage Guidance Council. Now, however, the word seems to be on everyone's lips and nowhere more often than in our universities and institutions of higher education. Scarcely a month seems to pass without students somewhere clamouring for a student counsellor or protesting at the inadequacy of the more traditional forms of pastoral care.

In such a climate the University of Keele has become the focus of considerable attention. Not only was it the first British university (together with Reading) to establish a counsellor training programme but it has for some years now been the only university in the country to operate a comprehensive counselling service for its own students staffed by counsellors who see themselves primarily as educators and only secondarily as therapeutic resource persons.

Those of us who work in the Appointments and Counselling Service at Keele are well aware of the growing interest in our activities. We are also conscious of the fact that there exists at present no account of what it actually feels like to be working as a full-time counsellor in a service such as ours. This book therefore is not intended as a scholarly contribution to the literature of counselling psychology, but rather as a descriptive record of what we as counsellors actually do at Keele, together with reflections on why we operate as we do and how it could be done better. There are times therefore when we hover somewhat uneasily between what really happens and what ideally could happen if we lived in a perfect world. And yet the ideal is for us only a possible vision because of our day-to-day experience.

Our hope is that such an account will be of interest to a

wide range of teachers and students in higher education and in sixth forms and that it may also serve a useful function in suggesting lines of thought to those who will be involved in the setting up of counselling services in their own institutions during the next decade. That such services will be established we have no doubt. The need is too great to go unrecognised for much longer.

We hope that the book will be of value to students of counselling and to the handful of counsellor educators who exist in this country at present. The transition from trainee to practitioner is often stormy and it may be that our account will assist by giving insight into the practicalities of the on-the-job situation. Finally we trust that the practitioners themselves will find something of interest in our reflections and we hope that some may be incited to criticise or oppose our ideas, for only in this way can further clarification and development of the counsellor's rôle come about. We feel fairly confident, at least, that they will breathe sighs of relief in sympathy with our unashamed admission of an imperfect eclecticism in the way we respond to the fascinatingly varied problems with which we are confronted from day to day.

PART ONE

CHAPTER ONE

Higher education and the counselling process

There are times when as counsellors we dread the chance encounter with a stranger at a party or in a train. So often such meetings result in the question: 'And what do you do?' To reply that one is a student counsellor by no means answers the question. On the contrary it produces looks of bewilderment and incredulity and further explanation is demanded. Not that we are incapable of defining our rôle but often we do so hesitatingly, for it somehow seems inevitable that we shall be misunderstood or, at best, only partially received. So often when we have said our piece the reaction is likely to be: 'Well, it all sounds very fine, but I can't understand why they need it. After all, in my day, we seemed to manage all right without having to go and cry on someone else's shoulder every five minutes. We're altogether too soft these days, we molly-coddle them too much.'

Counselling—an integral part of education

Such a response betrays a complete failure to understand the nature of the counselling process but, perhaps even more important, it shows an unwillingness to face the reality of society's present situation. This reality is such that it engenders the conviction lying at the heart of all our work—namely that counselling should be seen not as a frill or optional extra for those institutions fortunate enough to be able to afford a counsellor but as a central and integral part of the educational process for all students.

CHARACTERISTICS OF MODERN SOCIETY

In support of this view we would note the following aspects of contemporary society which go a long way towards defining the context in which our young people have to find themselves:

1. The world is considerably more complex than it was even ten years ago and the rate of change has never been greater. In occupational terms alone this presents today's student with a bewildering range of possibilities.

2. We live in an age when the certainties are gone and the authority figures of yesterday cut no ice. Increasingly we are having to learn to live with ambiguity, uncertainty and val·· confusion.

3. Our educational system—especially in its upper echelons—serves a competitive society but leaves little time for reflection or for the education of the feelings.

4. The drop-out rate in our universities averages about thirteen. per cent and it has been estimated that by 1980 twenty thousand could be dropping out each year. Current research points to the fact that in the case of students dropping out, over-persuasion to go to university in the first place, study difficulties, wrong choice of subjects, flagging interest and lack of concrete goals are clo. ly inter-related.

5. We have given the vote to the eighteen-year-olds and yet thousands of them—among them the most intelligent—have no constructive rôle to play in the development of our society. They remain financially dependent and often have no socially acceptable way of using the energy which they possess—all this at a time when further education is becoming increasingly the norm for the intelligent young person.

6. More perhaps than ever before young people are concerned about themselves and about their relationships. Some condemn this as selfish introspection. It is equally possible to see it as a genuine desire to come to grips with the underlying question in all human enterprises—the meaning of life itself, what am I here for, what can I do to justify my existence.

THE DEPRIVED ÉLITE

In such a society, and at such a time, the individual's potential for mental suffering is almost limitless and an inadequate form of education can render him horrifyingly vulnerable. In a strange way it also happens that the more intelligent the pupil the more unbalanced his educational diet can become. At the cognitive level he may well be stuffed with riches while his affective and social education are largely neglected or even deliberately ignored. We have found that the products of such one-sided education will often find their way to a counsellor early on in a university career.

Michael, for example, was a freshman who came to the Counselling Service in his first term because no matter how hard he seemed to try he could not settle down to work. He was falling badly behind with his essays and somehow nothing really seemed to interest him any longer. On exploration it turned out that Michael was really experiencing what we have come to recognise as 'eleventh hour awareness'. He had gone to a school where he had apparently been made to work very hard but where, as far as one could gather, there was little incentive to do much conscious exploration of his own needs and ambitions. It was assumed that intelligent pupils devoted themselves to A-level work with a view to entering university, and the whole ethos of the school unquestioningly reinforced this basic assumption. Michael's parents, too, were keen for him to do well and continually dangled the university carrot in front of his nose. The tragedy was that Michael had been very successfully conned by all this; he had accepted unhesitatingly the value system imposed upon him by others and had blindly striven to achieve those goals which others had established for him. What is more he had been successful—he got two B's and an A at A-level and came to Keele as a bright boy. It was only at the point when the supportive atmosphere of school and home was removed that Michael began to realise—very gradually and confusedly at first —that he had been deprived of the right of self-determination. Somehow he had never taken any of the decisions which controlled his life. He had not been given the chance to discover for himself the nature of his own thoughts and feelings, nor to examine his real needs let alone the variety of opportunities open to him. It was only his inability to adjust to the new university environment which revealed to him in how many ways his life had been subtly usurped. Having now to lead his own existence and make his own decisions he found that he did not know what he really wanted at all. He discovered, too, that he was socially inept and unable to communicate with the people about him; girls were particularly terrifying although he badly wanted a relationship with one. He found, too, that he had little motivation for academic work and that he had no idea of how to organise his own work programme or of how to cope with the apparently endless booklists.

B

Michael is a typical example of the deprived élite. He is one of those young people who, because of their intellectual capacities, are encouraged to direct their energy and devote most of their available time to the passing of academically demanding examinations. In the process such young people are often deprived of the opportunities to develop as emotional beings and have little chance of learning decision-making skills. Furthermore they do not have the satisfaction enjoyed by their wage-earning contemporaries of being financially independent and thus able to some extent to determine the pattern of their own lives. Allied to this there is often lurking just beneath the surface a profound fear. This fear is not easily analysed but it is concerned with meaning and with value. The young person who has had no time to explore himself and the world around him gradually finds himself confronted by disturbing questions about the validity of what he is doing and about his own value as a person. This will be the case especially if he lives in a community where he may perhaps have only the flimsiest of relationships with his contemporaries and perhaps none at all with adults apart from his parents— whose intrusion he anyway resents.

COUNSELLING AND THE EDUCATION OF THE FEELINGS

Counselling as we understand it, whether it be in schools or in higher education, is essentially concerned with these often neglected areas of a young person's education. Counsellors are educators who aim to create through the exercise of their skills an environment in which students can face and explore their own feelings without fear, learn how to cope more effectively with decision-making and examine their values and objectives without risk of condemnation. Additionally counsellors, if they are to be of maximum effectiveness in educational institutions, may well need particular expertise in such fields as study skills and vocational guidance.

The young person who is incapable of decision-making and confused in his own sense of values, will almost assuredly come to grief in a society which is increasingly demanding from him an ability to adapt confidently to rapidly changing circumstances. It is always difficult for the insecure person to cling on to traditional structures and patterns of behaviour without somehow sensing that he is evading the real issues and thus resigning himself to living only half a life. Counselling is essentially concerned with self-knowledge and self-determination and hence with fullness of living. It is not remedial treatment for lame ducks although it can sometimes take that form. Counsellors are not social workers nor are they welfare officers. They are educators. As such they believe that the educational process should be as much concerned with the pursuit of subjective as of objective truth.

Basic attitudes and the influence of Carl Rogers

To define the counsellor's rôle is not necessarily to throw much light on the actual counselling process and it is to this that we must now turn. Not, of course, that a simple exposition is possible. It would be naïve to suggest that counsellors can respond in the same way to all their clients. The student who is experiencing a severe emotional crisis clearly does not require the same handling as a man who is seeking help with essay-writing. Different problems will elicit different responses and call upon different facets of a counsellor's expertise. Nevertheless in our work at Keele it is undoubtedly true that we share a basic philosophy and orientation which form the context of all that we do. Much of this attitudinal stance derives either directly or indirectly from the theory and practice of counselling developed by Carl Rogers, the founder of so-called client-centred counselling. There is no slavish devotion and adherence to the Rogerian school but it is difficult to analyse our own operation without being immediately aware of Rogers' pervasive influence. For example, more than anyone else, he has come to define for us the sort of person we believe a counsellor should be.

THE COUNSELLOR AS A PERSON

This is not to suggest, of course, that there is a universal blueprint for the counsellor personality and it would be depressing if there could be. Nonetheless we have come to believe that there are certain characteristics which a counsellor must possess if he is to practise counselling as we understand it. In the first place he must be a man of faith—faith, that is, in his client's potential for growth. He must believe that change is possible and that this change can be effected not primarily by external pressures but by the efforts, with help, of the individual desiring it. There must be, too, a belief that man is basically a forward-moving, socialised, rational being who does not have a fundamental need to hurt either himself or others. On the contrary no matter whatever bitterness or hate may appear in behaviour the counsellor must believe that deep down in most individuals there is a constructive concern for others.

Secondly, allied to this belief, the counsellor requires certain personal qualities, or at least the ability to develop such qualities within himself. He needs to be warm, approachable, flexible, unafraid of experience and therefore able to incorporate data from his own day-to-day living. He must be spontaneous and genuine—prepared to enter the counselling situation as a person and not only as a rôle-playing professional. He must be accepting and non-critical of clients from a different age group and different backgrounds with different values and attitudes. He must be empathic—that is capable of sensing and understanding the client's private world as if it were his own but without being overwhelmed by it—and he must be able to communicate this understanding in language which the client can experience as appropriate and relevant to him. Finally he needs, if he is to be fully effective, a repertoire of specific skills, many of which we shall consider in detail at later stages of this book.

What counselling is not

To describe the counsellor is still not, however, to explore the counselling process itself although certain features of the process may now be evident by implication. At the risk of appearing perverse we shall further postpone this exploration by examining first some of the popular misconceptions of what counselling is all about. It is important, we feel, to expose these misconceptions, for they are often the result of the false expectations which others have of the counselling process. In such a situation there is always the danger that counsellors will be tempted to live up to the rôle which others have defined for them, however inappropriate it might be.

COUNSELLING IS NOT THE GIVING OF ADVICE

First, then, counselling is not the giving of advice or the supplying of recommendations. Such behaviour would run counter to the belief that individuals have within themselves their own resources for change and decision-making. Advice-givers derive much satisfaction from the activity for it enables them to feel constructively useful while at the same time allowing them to keep their own feelings of impotence safely at bay. Often, too, the advice-giver runs the danger of only half listening to the person in front of him. Before a problem has been half expressed he finds himself busily formulating plans for coping with it and as a result he cannot listen attentively to what follows. Part of the difficulty, too, will frequently lie in the client himself who will be only too anxious to place the counsellor in the rôle of advice-giver. All too often an interview begins with the words 'I wonder if you can give me some advice', and yet counsellors can be fairly certain that life for the person who is seeking help has been full of 'if-I-were-you' people and that they are unlikely to meet his need by simply putting on another performance of the same act, however impressive it might seem at the time. Counsellors are not concerned with impressing or directing their clients however strongly tempted they may feel on occasions to do both.

COUNSELLING IS NOT PERSUADING OR CONVINCING

Secondly, counselling is not influencing beliefs or behaviour by persuasion or argument or by attempting to convince, either directly or indirectly. This is a difficult lesson to learn for those counsellors who by the nature of their previous background and experience may have been mainly in a teaching rôle.

There are contexts, for example, where teachers and ministers of religion must quite legitimately seek to argue effectively and to formulate authoritative statements. The counselling situation, however, can very seldom permit of this. Once again, too, the client may be only too happy to collude with the counsellor who is tempted to take the persuader's rôle. Students especially are often very prone to remain at the cognitive level arguing into the early hours, and in the process successfully avoiding coming to grips with the essential element in their predicament which lies in the emotional area.

On rare occasions it may be necessary to engage a client at the cognitive discussion level before any real work can be done, but such discussion should be seen as a preparation for counselling and not as counselling itself. This does not imply that there is no place in counselling for intellectual, cognitive, rational factors. In our experience, however, such factors can normally only be viewed in the right perspective once the affective area has been opened up and explored. Furthermore, persuasion, argument and the like are usually guaranteed to bring about a situation where it is precisely the affective area that remains closed and un-investigated.

COUNSELLING IS NOT INTERROGATION

Thirdly, counselling is not interrogation. Counsellors in training commonly discover that they tend to fire a stream of questions at their unfortunate clients. As a result they often induce the kind of resistance which occurs when someone feels he is being attacked or diagnosed. The information gained in this way is consequently more than counteracted by the hostility engendered in the client. This resort to questioning often comes about because no other way of proceeding presents itself to the inexperienced counsellor and because, too, there is a tendency to believe that it is necessary to gather a mass of factual information about a person before he can really be helped. Social-work practice may be partly to blame for this with its emphasis on casework, which all too often seems to mean the compiling of an elaborate dossier of sometimes quite useless background information. Some theories of vocational guidance, too, are unhelpful in this respect with their emphasis on subjecting the client to a barrage of questions so that he can, with luck, be fitted into the right slot. But what-ever the reason for the tendency to interrogate it can fairly safely be assumed that the counsellor who catches himself posing more and more questions to his clients is not being very effective, and is not counselling.

COUNSELLING IS NOT PSYCHOANALYSIS

Finally, counsellors are not psychoanalysts. Carl Rogers tends to blur over the distinction between counselling and psychotherapy and perhaps he is right to do so, for it is frequently impossible to decide where the dividing line should come. On the other hand, counsellors need to be clear that their main area of concern will be with people who are experiencing normal developmental difficulties together with only a small number who are under-going moderate or even severe personality problems. They are bound, too, to be confronted at times by the more severe clinical disorders, but usually such cases will be beyond their competence and their main task will be to recognise this and to make the appropriate referral. Trouble can start if, instead, they embark upon a counselling session as if they were pale imitations of

Freud or Jung. If they do fall into this trap two things will almost
certainly occur. In the first place there will be a tendency to
persist in digging around in the past, especially into family
history, when this may well not be relevant, and secondly there
will be an over-eagerness to unearth the secret and unconscious
motivations of a client and offer interpretations of behaviour.
This is not to suggest that interpretation is always an inappropriate technique in counselling nor that counsellors should never
concern themselves with a client's family history. What we do
feel, however, is that counselling is not primarily concerned with
a reactivation of the past nor with that total re-education of the
personality at both conscious and unconscious levels which is the
rightful province of the psychoanalyst or the depth-psychologist.

Furthermore it is our growing conviction that analytically
trained counsellors are unlikely to fit happily into the kind of
service which we operate. If counselling is not psychoanalysis
neither are psychoanalysts likely to make effective counsellors as
we understand the rôle. The analyst's training equips him to deal
in depth over a lengthy period of time with the client who may
well, for example, be experiencing a degree of depersonalisation
which demands a radical reorientation of the personality. Such
training, however, is ill-suited to a concept of counselling such
as ours where the emphasis is on developmental needs and on the
continual interaction between the individual and the demands of
the institution and of society at large.

The counselling process—a shared enterprise

What then is the counselling process? Again, as with the counsellor
personality, there can be no universal blueprint and yet it is
worth while attempting to establish a model even if only to dispel
the mystique which so often surrounds therapeutic encounters.
Essentially the counselling process is concerned with change and
growth: but it is not the counsellor who seeks to change the
client. It is the client who seeks change and development within
himself and the counsellor's rôle is to aid such change not by
taking over direction for the client but by enabling him to clarify
goals and feelings to the point where he can confidently assume
self-direction. Clearly, therefore, the counselling process is very
much a shared enterprise. The client who expects the counsellor
to provide infallible solutions must quickly be disillusioned.

Instead he must gently be guided to the point where he can assume responsibility for his own life in full awareness of his own resources. But this is perhaps to jump the gun. What follows now is an attempt to provide in a simplified and idealised form a step-by-step account of the counselling process. Not all of it will, of course, be relevant to every case and perhaps very little indeed where a client's needs are highly specific or of a purely informational nature. Nevertheless it is hoped that certain basic attitudes will be evident which will be seen to obtain, no matter who the client is or how trivial his need may appear.

AN IDEAL MODEL OF THE COUNSELLING PROCESS

1. The person comes for help   He may come of his own accord or because someone else has suggested he should. In certain cases he may even have been told to come: if this is the case the counsellor needs to be fully aware of the fact if he is to cope effectively with the initial hostility which such pressure may have generated.

2. The counsellor attempts to relate to the client   The nature of this relationship is of crucial importance and if it goes wrong there will be little hope of achieving anything very constructive. The counsellor must convey, unselfconsciously, to his client a warm regard for him as a person of unquestionable value—he must convey, too, that he is willing for him to reveal his own feelings in his own way or, in other words, he must communicate his desire to help but not to control. Such acceptance is indicated by word, gesture, posture—by the total response of the counsellor to his client. Without it—and it is difficult to accomplish unless the counsellor actually likes his client—little growth will take place. If it happens, however, and the client does begin to experience that he is unconditionally liked and respected there is hope that he will then be able to face himself in the counsellor's presence without the fear which operates so strongly against the birth of insight.

3. The helping situation is defined   It is important to structure the counselling relationship at the outset by exploring what kind of help may be possible, what period of time is available, what sort of goals (however vague initially) can be established. This does much to rid the counsellor of an aura of omniscience with which the client may have invested him and it is helpful, too, in so far as it communicates to the client that there is a shared task ahead and that this will involve work and effort on both their parts.

4. The counsellor encourages his client to give free expression to his concerns   It is at this stage that the counsellor's ability to empathise with the client needs to be communicated if further progress is to be made. Unless the client feels that he is being received he will quickly lose confidence in the process and become reluctant to commit himself to it. At this juncture the counsellor's ability to reflect feeling accurately and to respond at the right level will be crucial. A more detailed discussion of the actual counselling skills involved in this operation appears in chapter four.

5. The counsellor accepts, recognises and helps to clarify negative feelings in the client   It is vital that the counsellor does not seek to evade his client's expression of fear, anger, depression, doubt or whatever it may be. Negative feelings need to be faced and vague reassurance at this stage can be positively harmful. Nor must they be cut short before they have been fully expressed. Clearly it is often painful to listen to a person denigrating himself or spelling out in detail the extent of his anguish or self-rejection but this must be endured if authentic growth is to take place later. It is usually the case that only when negative feelings have been fully explored can faint and hesitant expressions of positive impulses be voiced.

6.   The counsellor accepts and recognises positive feelings   In other words the counsellor's behaviour will indicate an understanding totally devoid of judgement. To call a person good can be just as threatening as to call him bad for it leaves the counsellor in the position of power, able to grant or to withhold approval at whim.

7. Development of insight   With a lessening of fear and anxiety insight should now be developing and the counsellor, by his responses, will try to aid the growth of self-acceptance which is the vital concomitant of awareness if behavioural change is to occur.

8. Establishing of new goals   With the development of more self-acceptance there will come an increased clarification of needs which will lead to the tentative establishing of new goals and objectives. It is possible at this point that the counsellor's rôle may take on a more directive or didactic flavour for the client may set up for himself goals which require for their attainment certain forms of expertise or information which the counsellor possesses. Obvious examples might be guidance in achieving more

effective study skills or authoritative information about an occupational area.

9. Growth of confidence and an ability to take decisions   At this point
the client will be initiating small but significant actions and will
need the counsellor's reinforcement and support. The counsellor
will be alert now for the moment when counselling sessions
should terminate.

It is perhaps worth remarking that with some clients stages 7,
8 and 9 may well be reversed. For many insight does indeed lead
to the establishing of new goals and the development of new
behaviours, but there are others for whom insight only follows
in retrospect. Such clients need to gain confidence by successfully
adopting more appropriate forms of behaviour before they can
come to a clearer understanding of their overall needs.

10. No more need for help   Ending a counselling relationship is not
always easy and the counsellor must beware of breaking off the
process prematurely. Usually, however, the client himself will
take the initiative, thereby giving further proof of his desire to
exercise his new-found autonomy.

Counselling and living in the present

It would, of course, be a marvellous world if every counselling
encounter proceeded in this exemplary fashion, but we hope the
idealised picture of a 'client's pilgrim's progress' will provide
some idea of the process which can and does occur. In some
cases the development may be very rapid (perhaps within two
sessions) while in others each step forward will be painfully slow
especially if the client needs to test a relationship in a hundred and
one ways before he feels able to trust it.

Finally, it is perhaps worth repeating again that this model of
the counselling encounter has little relevance in those many
instances where a student is, for example, merely seeking information or presenting a vocational query with little or no 'hidden
agenda'.

Such a global treatment of the counselling process leaves out
of account any exploration of the various skills and techniques
which the counsellor must possess if he is to operate effectively.
On the other hand, we hope that it is sufficiently explicit to
indicate the kind of attitudes and response to others without
which no amount of technical skill can lead to successful out-

comes. The counsellor must possess both the ability and the will to give himself to his client and to the counselling situation in such a way that the client can discover his own powers and achieve his own self-determination. Moreover, we become increasingly convinced that above all else the counsellor needs to live consistently in the present with his client. He requires a form of attentiveness which refuses to be distracted from what is actually taking place in the present moment. It is this, we have begun to feel, which constitutes the essential difference between counselling and other forms of helping relationship and therapeutic endeavour.

Our aim as counsellors must be the growth of our clients, but the way to that future end lies primarily in our intense involvement in what is presently happening within the private world of those who seek our help and within the relationship which we seek to establish with them.

CHAPTER TWO

The Keele Service in practice

The Keele Counselling Service consists of four full-time counsellors, a graduate administrative assistant and three secretarial staff. It has the responsibility of providing the conventional university 'Appointments Service' which is incorporated, unconventionally, into the global counselling function. We feel that it is impossible to divorce vocational concerns from the rest of an individual's potential personal needs. Getting a job, or, more euphemistically, choosing a career, is a hurdle faced by the vast majority of people and is an especially acute concern of most final-year undergraduates. In many cases it cannot be readily compartmentalised and is often completely entwined with other strands of personal-emotional concern.

We publicise the Service in various ways which are described in chapter three and it is entirely up to the students themselves to decide whether or not to use us.

DAILY ROUTINE

The Service is open five and a half days a week—Saturday mornings being primarily devoted to former students returning for help. The day is divided for each counsellor into seven sections each representing an hour's interview, four in the morning and three in the afternoon. The last hour of the morning and the first of the afternoon each day are allocated as 'on call' periods when urgent cases can be seen. Two counsellors each cover one of these periods each day. Counsellors hope to reserve one morning a week for private study. In practice, especially during full-term, it often happens that the pressures on the Service are such that this privilege has to be surrendered and the time spent seeing students or catching up on administrative tasks. The importance, however, of keeping abreast of developments in the counselling field is fully recognised and every effort is made to preserve these study periods from complete disruption. Half a morning each week is given over to a staff meeting in which departmental matters are dealt with ranging from discussion on who shall attend a particular meeting in a month's time to possible methods of handling a difficult client. The twenty-seven or twenty-eight sessions left for each counsellor are available for student interviews.

THE INTERVIEW AND ITS ENVIRONMENT

The interview 'hour' is an arbitrary span of time—it is rarely exceeded but sometimes it is considerably less. Our records show a range from five minutes to two hours: on most occasions a session lasts about fifty minutes. There is no predetermined limit to the number of interviews given to an individual student. This depends both on what the client feels he needs, and on what the counsellor feels the client needs, the only constraint being that no one student should monopolise a counsellor's time-table to such an extent that he causes a delay in others being seen. The frequency of visits is similarly determined: if a counsellor judges, and the client agrees, that there is a need for interviews to be held daily over a particular period of time, then this is what happens. The tables later in this chapter will give some idea of the distribution of interviews for each student.

Each counsellor has his own room which is of an adequate size and pleasantly decorated. It is left to the individual counsellor's taste how he adds to the furnishing of his room; pictures, book-cases and flowers are the usual embellishments. All the counsellors favour a face-to-face arrangement of comfortable armchairs without the barrier of an official-looking desk. Once the interviewing session is under way an unwritten but sacred rule ensures that it will not be interrupted except in an extreme emergency. External phone-calls are intercepted by a secretary on the master phone. Internal phones, with which each office is equipped, are fitted with a simple switch which enables the counsellor to substitute an unobtrusive, flashing light for the usual ringing tone.

REFERRAL ROUTES AND MAKING APPOINTMENTS

The routines by which students come to use the service are diverse. Many, however, come as a result of our invitations to them to meet us either in their first year to find out about our activities or to talk about their transition to university, or in their penultimate year, to explore career choices before entering the final year. Students take the initiative to use us at other times as they feel the need. Most of these are recorded as self-referred but it is not always possible to be sure that this is accurate. Many of them may well have been prompted to come by a friend or by a warden or tutor, but because we are not aware of this and make no point of asking, they are marked down for record purposes as self-referrals. Whatever the referral route, appointments are made either by telephoning one of the secretaries or by coming in to see them. Telephone numbers appear on our publicity handouts and are also in the university's telephone directory. The secretary responds to the request for an appointment by finding out whether the student wishes to see a particular counsellor. She also assumes responsibility for judging whether or not there is any urgency in the request: if she feels that there is she uses one of the 'emergency' times referred to earlier. If these are no longer available time will be made between two other sessions or at the end of the working day. Except in very busy periods even non-urgent clients are seen within a day or two of asking for an appointment.

RECORD KEEPING

Records are kept of every contact with a student in the form of case-notes which contain a brief description of each interview plus the reflections of the counsellor upon it. Record-cards for each student are also kept merely showing in coded form who saw the client, for how long, for what purpose and when. It is from these records, completed daily, that the tables which appear later in the chapter have been compiled.

For record purposes we have generated a number of problem categories to cover as far as possible the range with which we deal. It is worth listing them, with brief explanations where necessary, to indicate what we mean by the 'whole range of problems'.

1. *Subject choice* At Keele students do not have to decide upon their degree subjects until the end of their first, general year. Then two principal subjects must be chosen which will be studied to degree level—all Keele degrees being joint-honours degrees. There is little restriction on such choices, so that, for example, it is quite possible to take chemistry and economics, or psychology and French. In addition two one-year, subsidiary subjects must

be taken. As seventy-five per cent change their minds over one, originally intended, principal subject, and twenty-five per cent over both, it will be realised that such decisions preoccupy many students during their first year.

2. *Academic difficulty* This is distinct from the next category, study habits, and covers (*a*) those problems generated by a failure to cope effectively with a chosen course of study, arising, perhaps, from a disillusionment with the content of the subject, or with the way it is presented, or, even, with the personalities involved in its teaching, and (*b*) the fear, realistic or otherwise, of failing examinations in a subject or subjects which may or may not be intrinsically interesting to the student.

3. *Study habits* This category is concerned purely with difficulties in the mechanics of study. Thus such complaints as slow reading speed, inability to write essays, lack of sustained concentration, would all merit this label.

4. *Leaving* This covers those students who consult us on how actually to set about leaving the university for whatever reason, as well as those who seek information on the possibility of transferring to another university or to another institution of higher education. It is not intended that it should apply to those who have to leave involuntarily.

5. *General vocational information* This refers to those seeking information on the range of employment suitable to their particular academic and personal qualifications. It may also include discussion upon the whole process of applications for jobs.

6. *Specific vocational information* This is used when details of a particular area of employment, and of how to enter it, are required.

7. *Vocational indecision* Vocational guidance is often involved in this category pertaining, as it often does, to those who introduce themselves with 'I've got to get a job when I leave but I haven't a clue what I want to do!'.

8. *Personal* A global category subsuming problems of interpersonal relationships, of interaction with the institution, of marital and parental discord, of involvement with drugs. A category used, too, when the more dramatic, perhaps bizarre, psychiatric symptomatology is presented.

9. *Information* This excludes the vocational categories 5 and 6 and relates to all other types of information that may be requested: it may be for a statement, purely and simply, upon the

functions of our own Service; it may be for something rather more complex such as interpretation of a university statute.

10. *Concern about others*   Used when a student has felt the need to seek advice about the welfare of another person (friend or otherwise). It may be that the student has failed to be of any help himself, or that he does not know how he may begin to be of assistance, or he may be in doubt as to whether help is appropriate.

11. *Other*   The rag-bag into which otherwise uncategorisable difficulties have been put. These include some trivia, some unusual, even bizarre, encounters, and some unusual and serious requests for help.

Of course, such categorisation of interview material is artificial. In practice there is much overlap, so that, for example, it would at times be impossible to disentangle vocational indecision from personal, or academic difficulty from study habits. Our attempt to resolve this has been to record *all* categories that seem appropriate to describe the interview: our rule is, however, to put down first the 'presenting problem' that is, the difficulty the client initially expresses, in order for us to see just how and how frequently initially stated reasons for consulting us do in fact change or blur into other areas.

It is not intended to suggest that all the categories require the same amount of time and skill from the counsellor. For example, specific vocational information might require anything from a ten-minute discussion and the provision of a list of addresses of graduate recruiters in the computer industry to a series of hour-long sessions which lead to an examination of personal attributes and life-styles which might be expected of a teacher or of a marketing man. Again, it would not be impossible to have a student presenting a difficulty with, perhaps, the mechanics of studying history and after a matter of minutes to have the same student describing a set of symptoms which alert the counsellor to the possibility of an incipient psychosis. Such a case further demonstrates the need for great flexibility on the counsellor's part. (Readers who wish at this stage to acquaint themselves more fully with the actual range of counselling methods and techniques currently employed in the Service should consult appendix one on page 168 before proceeding further.)

Precise categorisation of the problem areas is made even more difficult by individual differences in the counsellors' perceptions.

There can be no clear-cut solution to the problem presented by the discrepancies, however minor, which inevitably result when four individuals attempt to identify and classify the nature of the interviews which they conduct. The possible sources of error must therefore be borne in mind when studying the following tables. Nevertheless, within their limits, these figures provide a valuable insight into the use that is made of the Service and of the nature of the clients who seek our help.

All figures are based upon the 1970–1971 academic year

TABLE 1

Students interviewed

	Men	Women	Total
1st year	76	75	151
2nd year	70	48	118
3rd year	104	73	177
4th year	152	113	265
Others	79	54	133
Total	481	363	844

TABLE 2

Number of Interviews

	Men	Women	Total
1st year	175	157	332
2nd year	272	132	404
3rd year	266	173	439
4th year	359	239	598
Others	130	153	283
Total	1202	854	2056

TABLE 3

Percentages of students interviewed

	Men	Women	Total
1st year	27	37	31
2nd year	29	30	29
3rd year	47	48	47
4th year	66	74	69
Total	42	47	44

TABLE 4

Percentages of students interviewed, (a) once only (b) twice

	(a) seen once only	(b) twice	a+b
1st year	56	25	81
2nd year	40	16	59
3rd year	57	24	78
4th year	52	25	78
Others	59	21	82
Total	53	22	75

TABLE 5

'Presenting problems' at first interview

	First year	Second year	Third year	Fourth year	Total	=	%
SVI	5	9	40	136	190	=	27
GVI	8	6	58	77	149	=	21
PA	24	44	32	12	112	=	16
L	52	23	4	4	83	=	12
IND	2	—	16	28	46	=	6
AD	7	17	12	1	37	=	5
SC	25	10	1	—	36	=	5
O	11	7	9	3	30	=	4
INF	13	—	—	1	14	=	2
SH	3	2	3	3	11	=	2
CAO	1	—	2	—	3	= —	1
Total	151	118	177	265	711	=	100

Key: SVI—requests for specific vocational information.
  GVI—requests for general vocational information.
    PA—personal adjustment problems, including difficulties in relation-ships with peers, tutors, parents or with the university system.
     L—wanting to leave or to transfer, usually asking for information on the procedures involved.
  IND—vocational indecision, including the infamous 'I've-no-idea-what-I-want-to-do' syndrome.
   AD—academic difficulty, which may, but not necessarily, include those who are failing academically.
   SC—subject choice. Students at Keele do not finally have to decide on their degree subjects until the end of their first year. Those

presenting this problem in later years are usually disillusioned by their choice and are contemplating transferring or repeating a year in order to read other subjects.

O—the category 'other', used when the problem fits nowhere else, e.g. 'Can I legally keep my non-functioning, un-taxed, un-insured car parked outside my home in London?'

INF—requests for non-vocational information, usually about the sort of services offered by counsellors.

SH—study habits—difficulties in the mechanics of coping with under-graduate work.

CAO—concern about others—usually a request for advice on how to cope with a friend or neighbour in distress.

CHAPTER THREE

Counsellors and the institution

A university counselling service must clearly be multidimensional if it is to meet all the needs of the potential clientele. This requires of the counsellors considerable flexibility of practice which would be unattainable if they saw themselves as adhering rigidly to a particular school of psychology or counselling. Nevertheless, as stated earlier, we do advocate what might be termed a humanistic Rogerian approach as a general basis for our response to clients. In line with this approach we believe that the counselling relationship should create the context in which clients can be enabled to achieve for themselves insights and solutions to their own problems. While this deprives the counsellor of the god-like charisma of the advice-giver it is more constructively useful, we feel, for him to act as a clarifier of difficulties and to allow his clients to explore their own thoughts and feelings and thus to arrive at their own conclusions whenever appropriate. Before the cynical critic objects, this does not mean that we only invariably and sagely utter 'uh-huhs' at intervals during our contact with clients. If someone asks for the address of a firm of accountants that employs graduates, then that is what he gets. If someone complains of his inability to organise his studies, then this difficulty is explored in detail and possible solutions (if any) are presented to him clearly and directly. If a client is displaying what the counsellor judges to be symptoms that can be effectively alleviated by chemotherapy then he is urged to consult the appropriate medical practitioner. If he is presenting a complex personal-emotional problem which seems to require the intervention of a psychotherapeutic skill possessed by the counsellor then this too is discussed openly and directly with him. None of these approaches are precluded by our Rogerian approach, only perhaps, by the ill-informed critic's mis-perception of what the approach entails.

A BACKGROUND OF FRIENDLINESS

The varying demands upon the Service which we have listed can, and we feel, should, be dealt with against an unchanging backcloth of friendliness which allows any client to retain his individuality and dignity. However superficial the client's problems there seems no reason why he should not be encouraged to relax and be allowed enough emotional elbow-room to state fully his particular difficulty or need. Such a basic attitude towards people cannot, of course, be artificially contrived, and will not therefore be a function of a counsellor's training or of his particular predilection for any school of psychological thought. It will be a measure rather of his humanity. Without this attitude there can be no counselling service as we know it.

We feel that this basic attitude should permeate the subsidiary aspects of a service. As far as space and money allow counsellors' rooms and waiting or information rooms, for instance, should be physically comfortable places for clients to be, and should offer no threat of public identification as 'cases'. There is every reason, for example, to provide easy chairs, newspapers, ashtrays and flowers in waiting rooms, or to provide a waiting room with a secondary purpose of, say, providing careers literature, so that the public eye is unable to discriminate between the client waiting to disclose some dark secret, and the client innocuously seeking information on Banking as a career.

Supporting staff are important as they are likely to have considerable contact, albeit brief and perhaps superficial, with clients. They, too, should be friendly and accepting, and ready to recognise and deal effectively with the agitated or tearful student.

In a way it may seem superfluous to be describing this sort of atmosphere. After all, what we are pointing out is simply that courteous friendliness should exist; a common enough condition one might think. But is it? We certainly find ourselves hard put to it to remember an institutional setting where this does invariably prevail. On the contrary, there are plenty of memories of waiting interminably and inexplicably in crowded waiting rooms where the very atmosphere is devoid of compassion and of respect for human dignity. Perhaps, though, we are advocating a cloyingly sentimental experience for our customers?

WHAT THE COUNSELLOR IS NOT

A keynote of warmth and informality is not achieved by magic. Clearly pressures on the space and time available to the Service will dictate to some extent its atmosphere. Of primary importance, though, as we have stressed in chapter one, is the personality, as displayed through his attitudes, of the counsellor himself. It is therefore with some alarm that we view the present rapid growth in this country of student counselling in institutions of higher education. There is little standardisation of recruitment and an even wider disparity between job specifications. In some cases a lone social worker is appointed to deal with an impossible potential case-load. Some appear to be taken on as a sop to vociferous student pressure and are expected to be counsellor, lodgings officer and teacher. Others seem to be glorified welfare officers and as such expected to dish out tea and 'never-mind-dears' to all and sundry. More commonly they are taken on as part of a medical service, and indeed, in some cases, medical practitioners themselves do the counselling. The, in our view, unfortunate aura of divinity which surrounds the medical profession in the eyes of many people, including the administrators of educational institutions when it comes to 'dealing with people', often leads to the conclusion that ill-health, both physical and psychological, is best left to the doctor. Doctors themselves rarely contradict this, and some would be very reluctant to admit that often they do not have the training, knowledge or skill to intervene constructively in some psychological disorders. Nevertheless a few would still ardently maintain that a person without a medical training should not have any therapeutic function at all. The more enlightened (increasing in number), admit that they do not have the monopoly of therapeutic skills, that counsellors, social workers and psychologists, too, have demonstrated that they can be responsible and knowledgeable enough to treat some disorders, even in some cases by methods developed in non-medical disciplines. Similarly it has become increasingly apparent that traditional psychotherapists and psychoanalysts are not essential for the relief of psychological stress. In our view medical practitioners have a necessary and crucial rôle to perform in an educational institution in their own right, and also by *supplementing* a counselling service as we shall see.

Without wishing therefore in any way to belittle the excellent work of those who have found themselves counselling in the situations described above, it is only honest to say at once that such models of the counselling function have little in common with the one we describe. It is doubtful, too, whether (even if so inclined) the counsellors involved could immediately attain a closer resemblance to our own particular model, depending fundamentally as it does upon autonomy within the institution.

When a counsellor is operating single-handed, or under the auspices of a medical service, experience shows that he will tend to attract to himself, or have referred to him, those clients who have already begun to think of themselves as in some way abnormal or disturbed: in just the same way people tend, on the whole, to go to the doctor when they believe they are sick—they conceptualise themselves as patients, or potential patients, before they even enter the surgery. It is clear therefore that a service which views counselling as desirable and appropriate for normal developmental problems must avoid at all costs this polarisation into a position where it is likely to be consulted only by those at crisis point or in extreme difficulty. At the same time, however, it must be seen as equipped to cope effectively with the more florid cases when they do arise.

SERVICE TO WHOM?

Given, then, our criteria of physical and emotional comfort, to whom are these facilities offered? Our assumption is that nearly every student and some staff too, will wish to make use of such a service's facilities at some time or other, and this does happen in practice. In any one year in our own Service we reckon to see nearly fifty per cent of the total population (of 2000) in the university. Nor is this surprising once it is remembered that as counsellors we view ourselves as educators and not as doctors or social workers. As we suggested in chapter one an essential part of a young person's educational development, we believe, is a growing capacity for self-awareness and an increasing competence in relationships, decision-making and in the establishing of realistic goals and values. Sometimes such development only takes place with much pain and confusion. It may even require a radical reappraisal of a whole mode of life. But more often the process is far less dramatic and occurs gradually and naturally enough during the course of a student's time in college. The counsellor's task, as we see it, is to aid this development in whatever way seems appropriate in each particular case.

Such, then, are our views of the essential elements in our model counselling service and of the nature of the population it should serve. Many implications emerge for its own internal structure, for its place in the institutional organisation as a whole, and for what is actually being offered as a counselling process. We shall look at these in turn.

PROFESSIONAL AND SUPPORTING STAFF

In the first place such a service must be generously staffed. It is disastrous to make false claims, and a service which professes to serve the whole community and then has a waiting list of weeks or months soon loses credibility. The work, too, is immensely taxing and counsellors who have to carry unreasonable case-loads soon cease to be effective with anyone. Exhaustion can lead not just to mediocre counselling but to positively harmful interaction. One sympathises especially with the solitary counsellor working in a vast institution without even a secretary. Supporting staff are vital, for they not only type letters and dispense information but help create the sort of environment already described. The counsellor who has to be his own receptionist, secretary, information officer and administrator is doomed to failure or worse. Supporting staff, too, reinforce the image of a service geared to the needs of the ordinary person, for they themselves are seen to be doing a normal job devoid of all the trappings of a medical or clinical mystique. At the same time, though, if they are properly selected and trained they are sensitive to the signs of extreme anxiety or tension and can do much by their behaviour to reassure a confused and frightened client.

THE GENERALIST COUNSELLOR

This concern to present an image of a service equipped to deal both with the normal and the exceptional can be reflected in many other ways. Most importantly, perhaps, the counsellors themselves should not be differentiated in terms of expertise. A student at Keele has a free choice of four counsellors and he has the right to expect appropriate help no matter whom he chooses or what his problem is. Clearly each counsellor has particular skills which his own interests have led him to develop, but this does not alter the basic principle that all the counsellors are generalists enjoying parity of esteem within the Service. This generalist quality is of crucial importance as it is common for a client to present what seems to be a straightforward informational or vocational problem only for this to be quickly dropped and replaced by a much more emotionally charged area of concern. A counsellor who is only competent in the vocational field, for example, would soon be floundering in such cases, and vice versa.

The place of vocational counselling in the overall work of a service is discussed in a later chapter, but it is worth remarking again that the whole operation of careers guidance does much to reinforce the image of a service meeting normal needs. Most people have to make vocational decisions and very often they require detailed information to help them in the task. Visually this has a profound effect on the Service's premises, when newspapers, reference books, information sheets, employers' literature and details of current vacancies are all very much in evidence.

Again, almost every student begins at some stage to question the effectiveness of his study methods and here, too, the willingness of the counsellors to explore such areas as reading skills, study techniques and note-taking, reinforces the image of a service catering for the needs of the average student.

On the other hand, where academic progress is hindered by so crippling a handicap as a phobia of small groups, it is most valuable if one of the counsellors can offer behaviour therapy to attempt to alleviate what is after all a relatively uncommon and distressing condition.

This generalist approach to a counselling service allows for the essential flexibility of doctrine which we have already stressed as being at the heart of the approach we are advocating. It is easily forgotten that in any one day a counsellor can be faced with as many different demands upon his expertise as he has clients. An inability on the part of the counsellor to make the appropriate shift of rôle, often in a matter of seconds or minutes, can only result in a sterile travesty of the profession of counselling.

MEDICAL SUPPORT

Lest it be assumed, however, that counsellors succeed in being all things to all men let it be firmly established, despite earlier remarks, that such a service could not function effectively and responsibly without the enthusiastic support and cooperation of the University Health Centre and without regular meetings with a psychiatric consultant. Such backing is vital, for without it counsellors might be tempted to trespass into territory beyond their competence or to give insufficient consideration to the possibility of physical disorder. There is all the difference in the world, however, between collaborating with a medical service and being part of such a service. The first guarantees the autonomy of the counselling service and allows it to serve the needs of the whole student body, while the second gives it an image with which only the more disturbed will identify, and thus obscures its relevance for the student population as a whole. There are other advantages too, to be gained from the existence of autonomous medical and counselling services. Most important, it enables the medical officer to make appropriate referrals in those cases where the problem is clearly non-physical, but it also enables counsellors to indicate on occasions that it is not necessary to be ill before making use of a medical service. At Keele, for example, it is not uncommon for a counsellor to refer a client to the Health Centre merely for a good night's sleep. The primary tasks of a medical service and of a counselling service are not the same, but where this is understood and the two willingly cooperate the benefits for the individual student can be enormous.

PSYCHIATRIC SUPPORT

The psychiatrist's rôle is equally vital to the effective work of counsellors, for he provides the kind of safeguard which often makes it possible for them to remain confident in stressful situations. The knowledge that a referral can be made easily and speedily if this seems appropriate has a powerful influence upon a counsellor's responses to a clinically disturbed student. The burden of having to bear ultimate responsibility can have a totally disastrous effect on the counsellor's handling of a case whereas the knowledge that the responsibility can easily be shared with or handed over to a doctor or psychiatrist simply by lifting a telephone, often alleviates the counsellor's own anxiety and releases him to do some of his best work. Not that the counsellor should feel himself to be a mini-psychiatrist who needs 'Big Daddy' to turn to when the situation gets too hot. Counselling is a skill in its own right but it is not psychiatry. Even though the counsellor must have an appreciation of, and be able to recognise, psychiatric symptoms, and sometimes even actively 'treat' some well-defined psychiatric disorders (see chapter four) he cannot and certainly should not have any pretensions towards being a psychiatrist. Those who do, perpetrate an unsavoury injustice both to psychiatry and to counselling.

The psychiatrist, although often untrained in counselling skills and techniques, is an expert in psychiatric diagnosis and treatment. Trouble can really begin for the client when a counsellor attempts to work in depth with someone who is, in fact, suffering from a clinical illness. A service which has effective psychiatric support is unlikely to fall into this trap.

Coordination can also be of advantage to the psychiatrist, for he is unlikely to spend a disproportionate amount of his time seeking to help persons with developmental difficulties when he can refer them for appropriate help to a counsellor, and he might well be relieved to find that there are other professionals to whom he can refer. In our own experience some clients derive considerable reassurance from a psychiatric interview which results in them being referred back to a counsellor, for they are released from the fear of mental illness and can then use the counselling situation with renewed hope and determination. This is but another example of cooperation between counsellors and other professionals, working to the best possible advantage of an individual student. Such an outcome would be less likely, we feel, if the counselling service did not enjoy its own autonomy and define its own aims in terms of its particular contribution to a student's education.

CONFIDENTIALITY AND RELATIONSHIPS WITHIN THE INSTITUTION

No student would use a counselling service unless he had confidence that the counselling interview would be conducted in the strictest confidentiality. At the same time, however, this rule of the secular confessional can lead to an aura of mystery and even furtiveness about a counselling service's activities unless its rôle is accepted and understood by the institution as a whole. This is not easily achieved, for such communication has to proceed in several directions simultaneously. A counselling service in a university cannot, for example, simply confine its attention to the student body, for its effectiveness with students will be greatly influenced by the attitudes of academic staff, welfare staff and administration. Counselling in institutions involves an understanding of the dynamics of the institution itself and an awareness of how these impinge upon the well-being of individual members of the community. The implications of this are considerable and we propose to explore some of them as they affect the counselling service's relationships with, first the student body, second the academic staff, third the welfare staff and finally with the administration.

RELATIONSHIP WITH THE STUDENT BODY

When they arrive in higher education very few students will have had experience of counsellors and counselling. This means that a counselling service is faced with the considerable task of publicising itself and interpreting its function to the student body. To this end we have tried a number of methods at Keele with varying degrees of success. An explanatory leaflet, describing the Service in some detail (see appendix two), is sent to all freshmen before they come to the university, but clearly this will mean little to many students at so premature a stage. In recent years we have held open seminars during the freshmen's reception period during which we have attempted to illustrate the Service's function by means of taped extracts of rôle-played interviews. This method seems to have been fairly successful and certainly excited considerable comment and debate both at the time and afterwards. A little later on, once students have had a chance to find their feet, we issue invitations to everyone in the first year to come and meet with us individually—or in groups if they prefer—so that we can have a further opportunity of explaining to them the nature of the service we offer and of showing them around the Careers Library. In these various ways we feel reasonably confident that we make ourselves known to about eighty per cent of the annual intake and it is not uncommon as a result for freshmen to be making use of the Service within the first week or two of their time in the University. Some, of course, slip through the net but even those students who have had no direct contact with the Service (and possibly want none) are likely to know of our existence through friends, through references in other orientation lectures, or through university publications.

No amount of publicity, however, will inspire confidence of its own accord. The task of building up student trust in the integrity, professional competence and general effectiveness of the Service is an infinitely more complex one. Most students, for example, are anxious about assessment and often they fear that exposing weaknesses will prejudice their chances of gaining favourable judgements from their academic tutors. For this reason the issues of confidentiality and the neutrality of counsellors are of paramount concern. Experience reinforces strongly our belief that confidentiality must be absolute and that counsellors should not be involved in the academic teaching or assessment of students. This is not to maintain that effective counselling cannot be done by members of the teaching staff but as we have said before such people may well experience, or create for the student, a confusion of rôles which makes it difficult to establish the kind of relationship where counselling is likely to be most successful.

A student for example can be in the invidious position of at one minute being treated with concern and sympathy over some academic difficulty, and at the next being told fairly smartly that if there is not a dramatic improvement in his work the consequences could be serious for his future in the institution. The resulting confusion is not likely to endear the 'counsellor' or the teacher to the victim. Even worse is the situation where the counsellor-teacher feels compelled to 'report' a client's misdemeanour to the 'appropriate authorities', either telling or not telling the client beforehand. A client faced with this situation has every right to feel that the attempts to help him constitute a ludicrous confidence trick. There is no substantial reason why a counsellor cannot operate confidentially, even though this may well be one of the things he has to uphold in the face of more virulent critics. This does not necessarily mean that a counsellor *never* conveys any information about a client to anyone else. Where he feels that it can be a positive help to a solution of a problem then it is incumbent upon the counsellor to put this to the client. In our experience, whenever this has been done the client has invariably concurred.

If the principle of confidentiality fails to be upheld the clientèle of the service, almost certainly, will, and should, rapidly dwindle. As students appear to be becoming increasingly politically conscious little faith will be put in a service which appears to collude with the authority figures of the institution. Nor again is a counselling service likely to be able to function effectively if it is held in low esteem by student leaders. For this reason and for many others, too, we have found it desirable and often highly productive to meet regularly with the elected representatives of the Students' Union. Such occasions give student leaders an opportunity to express their current concerns and plans for the student body and they also give counsellors the chance to feed back ideas which have a bearing on the mental health of the community as a whole. Most important of all, however, is the fact that such meetings throw student leaders and counsellors together in a friendly working relationship which does much to promote positive attitudes towards the rôle and aims of the Counselling Service throughout the University.

RELATIONSHIP WITH ACADEMIC STAFF

Academics are not, necessarily, outstanding examples of emotional maturity. A life devoted to the pursuit of scholarship and intellectual excellence does not always lead to the evolution of a well-balanced personality. It is likely therefore that for many academics the counsellor's concern with emotional growth will be misunderstood and even feared and his relevance to a university setting at all may well be questioned. Not, of course, that this is true of all academics or indeed of the majority. In very many cases tutors and professors are vividly aware of the problems and difficulties which beset their students and hinder their intellectual development. Frequently, too, they are uncomfortably conscious of their own powerlessness to respond to this kind of need.

The counsellor in his relationships with academic staff has a delicate path to tread. In the final analysis he must prove his usefulness and this will be apparent by the way in which he enables students to take proper advantage of the academic opportunities presented to them. But in doing this he must be sure not to trespass on the often precious relationship between a teacher and his pupil, nor must he appear to be abrogating to himself certain teaching functions which the academic may rightly regard as his own. In this respect help with the acquisition of appropriate study skills for example can sometimes be misunderstood, although there are in fact few academics who are experienced in this field. More elusive considerations are involved, however. Counsellors, if they are to win the acceptance of academic staff as educators with special skills, must inspire confidence at the intellectual level. They probably need to be graduates who feel comfortable in intellectual discussion and who have the assurance which springs from specialist knowledge and competence. The counsellor who is always on the defensive or even feels intellectually inferior may well find himself written off before he has had a chance to give instances of his usefulness. It also follows that counsellors cannot be content to remain in their offices counselling students. They should be prepared, if asked, to give public lectures on their specialisation and on other related matters, and they should also be seeking every opportunity to increase their own professional competence and knowledge. They have a responsibility, too, in the area of research. An effective counselling service will be concerned to monitor its own operation and this should result in research papers and articles which are of immediate interest to academic staff. We are not suggesting here that counsellors should attempt to beat academics at their own game. Rather we are saying that a counsellor's ability to establish good working relationships with academic members of staff will largely be determined by his own intellectual stature and by the evidence he provides of professional skill and knowledge, and by his willingness to be open about what he does.

Good relationships with academic staff are particularly crucial if students are to be helped effectively. In the same way, for example, that students are unlikely to consult a counsellor if the image of the service is bad, so, too, academics will be unlikely to refer students to counsellors if they have little respect for either the personalities or the professional competence of the counsellors in question. It often happens that a student's problems are either the direct outcome of academic situations or at least exacerbated by them. In these cases it is often sensible, with the student's express permission, to involve academic members of staff in some form of social engineering which may well profoundly alter a student's response to his predicament. Such intervention would be very difficult to accomplish if academic members of staff were unwilling to accept counsellors in what amounts to a consultancy rôle. Our experience suggests, however, that when confidence is established faculty members are often prepared, under a counsellor's guidance, to go to great lengths to improve a student's learning situation and thus to increase enormously his chances of completing his course successfully. For example, a department at Keele was prepared to provide individual tutorials for a girl while she was being helped by a counsellor to come to terms with her great anxieties about group work: and on another occasion a student with obsessional perfectionistic traits was allowed at a time of crisis to present his notes instead of a completed essay which he had begun and torn up a dozen times.

RELATIONSHIP WITH WELFARE STAFF

The point of view has sometimes been expressed to us that counsellors might expect to find themselves readily accepted by many academics who are, after all, interested in having enthusiastic, hard-working students as free from neurotic and study problems as possible. The opposition, it is maintained, will surely come from those handful of dons and others who are more than averagely interested in student welfare and student problems—that is to say those who have quite specific pastoral rôles—such as wardens, resident tutors, chaplains and those personal tutors for whom the job is more than an additional chore.

It would be foolish to pretend that there is no truth in this particular supposition. Clearly there is almost certain to be some suspicion and even jealousy from welfare staff who, while not professionally trained, believe that they have an important contribution to make to a student's happiness and well-being. The situation is not helped at the present time by the growing distrust in student circles of the worthy amateur who brings with him the aura of a paternalism which is now strenuously resisted in almost all spheres of student life. The rôle of the warden, for example, presents particular difficulties. There was a time until quite recently when the warden of a hall of residence had a fairly well-defined function. He aimed not only to be a student's friend and adviser but he also had the responsibility for the overall administration of the hall and for upholding the rules of the institution. In fact, he was both a welfare officer and to some extent a disciplinary figure. This latter rôle, if it has not altogether disappeared, is now under heavy fire. In many colleges students draw up their own rules and regulations, hours rules and the like, and the warden has become little more than an arbitrator when there is internal strife among the members of a hall. What authority is still retained is often more on paper than in reality. It can be argued that such a development releases the warden and resident tutors to become wholly welfare orientated but this is not always easy for staff who have lived for years under a different dispensation.

Our experience is making it increasingly evident, however, that the establishing of a professional counselling service need not, and should not, mean the eclipse of other welfare functions. On the contrary, counsellors can release wardens, chaplains and others from the fear of over-involvement in the same way that they themselves are granted greater freedom of action by psychiatric support. A warden is more likely to respond to the needs of a distressed student when he knows that he can consult with a counsellor or, if it seems necessary, actually refer him for more skilled help to the counselling service without in this way labelling the student a psychiatric case. Nor is there any reason why counsellors and other welfare staff should find themselves in conflict. On the contrary, our experience suggests that the presence of a counselling service affords welfare staff the chance to improve their own expertise through seminars, group discussion and informal consultation. Counsellors, if they act sensitively and diplomatically, can aid other welfare staff to re-define their rôles in a changing society and enable them to become more effective in their interaction with students. We discuss this whole question of cooperation and rôle definition in part three. Suffice it to say at this point that if the presence of a counselling service means less involvement with students by other members of the staff, whether academic or welfare, then something is badly wrong with the counsellors. The same, incidentally, can be said of a school counselling service, although it would seem that the initial enmity from teachers with pastoral care responsibilities towards a school counsellor can be far greater and far more irrational than anything we have experienced in the university setting.

RELATIONSHIP WITH ADMINISTRATION

Vice-chancellors, registrars, principals and other leading administrators are unlikely to be much envied at this period in the history of higher education in Britain. We have not yet reached the position of the U.S.A. where dozens of college presidencies remain vacant because nobody dares take on the task. There is little doubt, however, that the hot seat could become even hotter during the next few years as the ferment about almost every aspect of education continues. Student leaders will not allow dons to become complacent now that student participation in university government has been partially achieved. There are almost certain to be greater struggles ahead over curriculum reforms and social involvement. Certainly, for many students, the very

c

existence of an élitist university or college presents complex problems in which they are intimately involved. Such questioning can lead to an almost total value confusion where all presuppositions have to be thrown back into the melting pot and painfully re-examined. For some it means being adrift for a while on an ocean of seemingly endless relativity where nothing can be regarded as absolute.

Such an atmosphere breeds unrest, political agitation and even violence. In such times counsellors are bound on occasion to come under attack from administrators who see them perhaps as colluding with the hotheads and the disturbed revolutionaries who are welcomed like everyone else into the confidentiality of the counselling interview. Such criticism must be tolerated even if by so doing a counselling service puts its own existence in jeopardy, for if it is once rumoured among the student body that counsellors are time-servers devoted to the maintenance of the status quo or, worse still, to the task of adjusting students to the institution, then all credibility will be lost. We believe that in such a situation the absolute confidentiality of a counselling service, by proclaiming the counsellor's commitment to the individual, actually works towards the greater health of the community as a whole. Much current unrest in universities may well be attributable to disturbed students acting out their 'hang-ups' at the community level. Counsellors, by providing the opportunity for such students to explore their difficulties in a less public setting, will not prevent protests, sit-ins and the other manifestations of student discontent. On the other hand, they may well be helping towards a state of affairs where such demonstrations are purged of the elements of sick aggression which must inevitably lead to destructiveness rather than to creative reform. It is also possible that counsellors with their emphasis on personal growth and individual need may indirectly promote the revolutionary insight that vice-chancellors and principals too are human.

WHO SHOULD ACTUALLY EMPLOY THE COUNSELLORS?

We are often asked whether counsellors ought not, more appropriately, to be employed by students' unions rather than by the educational institution itself. We feel strongly that such an idea springs from a false understanding of the counsellor's rôle. The counsellor as educator has a responsibility to the whole community and not only to the student body. Furthermore it is unlikely that he will be able to serve even a student's best interests if he is divorced from the academic and administrative staff and is seen simply as an advocate for the students' union. It is no good a counsellor having the ear of the student president if he has no ready access to the vice-chancellor or to the professors. There is also the additional problem of financial support. The students' unions are never affluent and many are in the red. It is unlikely therefore that they will be able to afford the kind of salary which will attract a suitably qualified and experienced person, nor is it likely that they will be able to afford the necessary supporting staff. Finally we are doubtful whether a counsellor appointed and financed by students would in practice inspire the same kind of confidence among the student body itself, as an independent professional service financed by the institution but clearly seen to be serving the needs of individuals within that institution. In a curious way students are often mistrustful of the very services which they themselves have established.

PART TWO

CHAPTER FOUR

The counselling process—what actually happens

What actually occurs in the encounter that we call counselling? This has been partially answered in part one when we described a basic approach of concern and physical comfort. Now we attempt to illustrate what actually happens within the isolation of an hour's counselling session.

A COUNSELLING INTERVIEW: I

Let us begin at a beginning. A normal working day, with a second-year student, Dave, booked in to see me at, say, 2.15 that afternoon. I know his name but little else, apart from the subjects he is reading. From our records it is clear that this will be his first visit. From the secretary who made the appointment I find out that he did not mind which counsellor he saw, and that he did not sound particularly upset, nor for that matter, particularly cheerful.

He arrives on time, I introduce myself and take him into my room, we sit down and I say 'well, how can I help?' He seems slightly nervous, shifts his position and replies a little ruefully 'I don't know that you can really. It's just that a friend of mine told me to come here; I don't think I'm mad or anything—though sometimes I wonder—it's just that everything seems, oh I don't know, pointless I suppose.' And here he seems to stop, sheepishly. Even though I still know very little about either him or his problem I could at this point make any number of responses ranging from 'have you seen a doctor?' through 'what do you mean "pointless"?' and 'you say you sometimes think you're mad?' to 'go on.' Any of these might possibly be either appropriate or disastrous depending upon the tone in which they are uttered and whether this is in harmony with the physical presence of the counsellor. I might make the response 'you say you sometimes think you are mad' in an incredulous manner and risk engendering considerable hostility; or I might say the same thing in a concerned tone establishing some sympathy for him, but I might say it in this way while gazing distractedly out of the window or concentrating on the doodles I am sketching, so that any verbal sympathy emanating from me is considerably diluted. In short, whatever I say, if anything at all, at this point, must manifest both my attention and my concern. I shall be looking at him and I shall not be bodily restless. Moreover, this will not be some sort of act, I shall express these things implicitly because he *is* holding my attention and because I *am* concerned.

In fact I am not particularly interested in making any sort of response at this point in the interview. I want him to express himself, as I am not yet in any position to understand, to assess or to diagnose his troubles. Anything I do say will be designed to encourage him to continue talking. If the silence following his initial statement seems to be uncomfortable for him then I suspect I am most likely to say 'go on' in as encouraging a way as possible (I do not conceive of using the question 'have you seen a doctor?' despite having said earlier that it might be a possible alternative!). I want whatever feedback he is getting from me—a stranger who might help him—to be at least neutral and as non-negative as possible. We are, after all, but a minute or two into the session.

Let us assume that I have said 'go on' to break the silence. Then—

'Well . . . it's so difficult to put into words. See, I came from school, really looking forward to university. Keele was my first choice because of the Foundation Year, and everything was great, I really enjoyed it. I made a lot of friends and I got good marks in most of my work. Fantastic. And this year started off the same: but, I don't know, I came back after Christmas and just felt down, cheesed off. It wasn't just me either. The whole group of us seemed to get on each other's nerves. I thought it would just be a passing thing, but it's been three months now and it's getting worse. The rest seem to be managing all right, but me . . . well . . . I've never been like it before, everything's so dreary . . .' And so into another silence, not uncomfortable this time, more a period for thought which he breaks with 'the worst of it is that now I'm really falling behind with work . . .'

But before we continue let us enter the counsellor's mind while this was taking place. Apart from listening intently, and occasionally nodding and grunting understandingly and involuntarily he is also assessing, judging, and raising questions to himself so that when he does respond it is unlikely to be in a purely spontaneous way and may be for very precise reasons indeed. So—'he seems at home now and only too ready to talk about himself. I'm going to have to watch the time and I don't want him to begin rambling, though I don't think he will. I wouldn't be surprised if this gets pretty emotional—he's really listening to himself with a sort of shock. God, I wish I hadn't got John at 3.00, he's always early. I don't think he's really depressed, seems alert and talking coherently enough. Should I get into his daily routine? Is work really suffering? Is he sleeping O.K.? Still got his friends? Yes, I suppose one sent him here—wonder who that was. Shall I ask about his work now? No. I want to hear more now he's got the bit between his teeth.' Back to Dave with—

'The worst of it is that now I'm really falling behind with work, just doing the minimum and that not very well . . . It's not that I haven't got the time, I don't do anything all day, I can just about drag myself to tutorials, and then it's drinking coffee and listening to records . . . It's such a bloody waste of time I've even thought of packing it all in—I haven't got the energy to do that . . . You must think me an awful twit, I'm sorry I know there's nothing *you* can do.'

He stops abruptly here, as though he has asked the direct question as to whether I can do anything about it.

This part has taken some time to express and Dave would seem to have decided that there was little more to say now that he has stated his problem. During this part the counsellor becomes surer in his categorisation of Dave's problem—'so he *is* getting *some* work done. I think he's asking to be taken over, given direction. Has he *really* thought of leaving? Ask him. Here's the crunch. Shall I tell him what sort of help I can give? No, let's see how bad it is for him. What shall I say then? 'I don't think you're a twit'? I don't want a long silence to develop here, that would be too dramatic. I must pick up the challenge. Oh! Come on, think quicker. Right. 'It's interesting that you say there's nothing *I* can do, because you sound pretty much at the end of your tether at dealing with it yourself.'

> *Dave:* I'm that all right . . . there isn't much you can do is there, I mean it's up to me. I know what's wrong—I'm lazy. It's up to me to . . .
> *Counsellor:* So it's a trivial problem after all?
> *Dave:* No, but you can't . . .

> *Counsellor:* Yes, you're right of course. Well, half right perhaps. I certainly can't, and wouldn't want to, sort of, get hold of you by the scruff of the neck and somehow *make* you work and be more cheerful. But by coming here you're saying 'isn't there anything I can do?' and I want to say that perhaps there is something we can do together, that perhaps we can try out some new approaches.
>
> *Dave:* Anything . . .
>
> *Counsellor:* You really said that in a heartfelt way.
>
> *Dave:* You've no idea how pissed off I am with myself! Just the thought of there being a way out feels good.
>
> *Counsellor:* O.K. Dave.

During this section, which has passed quite rapidly, the counsellor has had little time for detailed contemplation as he is actively engaged in conversation. Now though, he has offered something of a contract by stating the possibility of a successful joint enterprise. He has become surer that what is being presented is a situational difficulty as opposed to a clinical problem and he is likely to work upon that assumption until some evidence suggests otherwise. Two avenues of exploration have opened up, his work difficulties and the breakdown of relationships. Having, as it were, skirmished and attained a fair degree of rapport the scene is set for some detailed work on both these areas. Which to choose first is a matter of chance. What does seem clear is that there is not going to be enough time to complete this phase so that a further session is going to have to be offered before the close.

So with the businesslike 'O.K. Dave' (which also acknowledges the relief expressed by him) the counsellor goes on:

> 'Why don't we look a bit more closely at the work situation? You say you're just lazy but you are also pretty worried by it.
>
> *Dave:* Well, I just don't seem able to get down to it. As I said I go to lectures, then I go over to the Union and have a cup of coffee. Then I think, well, it's not worth doing much before lunch, so I just sit around and read the paper, have food, go back to my room, listen to records. Then I'll start to think 'Christ! I'd better do some reading for an essay', but that's as far as it gets, and I think I should get up and do something about it but I don't so I get really cheesed off with myself then, but I say to myself I can do it later on— And so it goes on . . .

I don't know . . . then I get really depressed and wonder if it's all worth anything . . . I mean . . . well, I haven't got any real friends or anything, so I don't . . . well I mean, I can't . . . I don't know . . .

Counsellor: No one to talk to.

Dave: No, not really. And I suppose that's it really. (Pause)

Counsellor: (Gently). So what are you saying, Dave? that you haven't any real, close friends, that being cheesed-off really means you're lonely?

Dave: (who doesn't answer for what seems a very long time, and is perhaps a minute, and who seems close to tears).

Again let us leave the interview to indicate what seems to be happening. This phase began in a workmanlike manner with the aim of getting down to looking at the work situation. In a short time Dave seems to be expressing an underlying concern—his lack of friends. The counsellor could have ignored this in order to exploit his stated theme of 'the work situation' instead of which he tracks what he senses to be important feelings that are being expressed via the hesitancy. In the counsellor's mind during this portion of the session might be:

So—'it's a work-anxiety vicious circle. Shall I get him to fill in a schedule of his days' activities? No, no point. Got to end soon. There's a hell of a noise outside. Brian's bloke sounds cheerful. Come on Dave, what's the matter? Listen. 'No one to talk to!' I should have got here before. No maybe not. Forget it. He's lonely. I'm too tense. Wait—Your voice is going to sound odd. Relax. Now. 'So what are you . . . saying Dave? That you haven't any real, close friends, that being "cheesed-off" really means loneliness?' That's better. Comfortable now. What's he going to say? I can't end yet. I'll have to get him back later: what's on at 4.00? It must be today. Where will we go from here. It's all right though, we're together.'

Let us assume that the session ends ten minutes later. With little drama an appointment is arranged for 4 o'clock that afternoon. Dave has, as it were, confessed to an inability to establish relations with other people and has agreed to explore this further.

What are counselling skills?

This, then, has illustrated in a necessarily cumbersome way the sorts of activity that might take place. It illustrates, too, what we have alluded to in earlier chapters as 'flexibility'. This may now be seen as a sort of sensitivity to changes in the substance of the client's expressions: the counsellor's ability to change course abruptly when it seems necessary even though it might mean frustrating the development of a theme that the counsellor himself is comfortable with and feels to be useful. The judgement 'when it seems necessary' is based upon the fundamental assumption that it is the client's expression of feeling that is of paramount importance: that one is in business as a counsellor not to tell people what it is that they should be revealing, but to allow and to facilitate the fullest expression of the client's own difficulties. As we have said before, there are plenty of people—friends, teachers, parents—who, in attempting to help with personal problems, sincerely and naturally restate these problems by inferring that they are similar to the ones that they themselves have experienced and may be resolved by similar methods. This leads to the well-meaning but usually inappropriate 'if I were you . . .' or 'I had the same trouble and what I did was . . .' kind of response. By avoiding this and aiming at as comprehensive a statement of a problem area (which may in itself be a protracted process and not be conveniently done in ten minutes or an hour) the counsellor is distinguishable from the friend, or the neighbour. This sort of relationship, simple-sounding as it may be, is a rare occurrence in the myriad relationships which constitute a person's day-to-day social interactions.

And it *is* surely 'simple sounding'. After all what we are so far claiming as counselling skills are (*a*) the ability to listen carefully to what is being expressed; (*b*) the ability to resist intruding with our own interpretations, our own attitudes or our own reminiscences immediately they occur to us; (*c*) the ability to restrain oneself from physical and verbal manifestations of disgust or contempt or boredom or humour at what we are being told; (*d*) the ability to respond in ways which are likely to encourage the fullest disclosure of our clients' difficulties, that is, by demonstrating verbally or non-verbally our interest, our concern and our comprehension of what is being expressed; and, (*e*) ability to match the impression that we are building up of the person and his problem against those which constitute well-defined clinical or sub-clinical syndromes. It is often argued that with the possible exception of (*e*) these hardly warrant the term 'skill' or 'ability'; that these are the usual ways in which people operate in everyday interpersonal encounters; that one is trying to sanctify a rather mundane set of procedures. Just as we felt it necessary to spell out the importance we attach to the physical comforts of our waiting-room and the friendliness of our supporting staff, so we feel it necessary to do the same with a description of counselling skills. In our experience these are *not* by any means universal skills, nor are they universal within the so-called 'caring' professions. Shortage of time is often given as the reason why such 'skills' are not manifested more frequently by 'caring' professionals. This is obviously true in some cases, but in most we are forced to the conclusion that whether such abilities are innate or acquired most people do not possess them; many just do not want to possess them and are not prepared to cultivate them, often on the grounds that it is faintly ridiculous to treat people in such a benign way, for it achieves even less than the stern man-to-man, pull-yourself-together, confrontation. Others feel that some stricture must be imposed at least initially, that one must straightaway obtain a detailed family, educational and medical history. We do not condemn such views unless it is maintained that they must be put into practice on every occasion regardless of what the client presents, when there would seem to be nothing to commend them except insofar as they might make the counsellor feel good. Similarly we do not want to suggest that the sort of verbal interaction illustrated earlier should always prevail, even within a series of interviews with the same person. The categories of skills listed above may be seen very much as tools, each one, or each possible combination, having a specific application. Choosing which to use is obviously a matter for professional judgement which itself may be measured by the facility and confidence with which the practitioner selects and implements the different possible approaches, and by the flexibility he displays in modifying his approach whenever appropriate in any single encounter.

A COUNSELLING INTERVIEW: 2

What, for example, might have been good for the encounter with Dave may well be quite incongruous with the next client of the day, Shirley, who starts with

'I won't keep you long, but I'm pretty sure I want to do post-graduate work in philosophy and I want to know how to set about it.'

Any initial response from the counsellor other than a direct factual answer, at worst, confessing his ignorance, at best detailing the procedure of selecting and applying for such places, would be embarrassingly inappropriate. Even so a purely informational reply can be conveyed with all sorts of meta-messages by tone of voice, gestures and posture of 'don't-bother-me-with-such-trivia', or of 'you've got a hope!' or perhaps 'nothing could be simpler, you're as good as there'. Assuming that the counsellor is able to provide accurate information without arousing the hostility or false expectations of the client, whether he then goes on to widen the scope of the interview is going to depend upon both the client's apparent willingness to do so, and upon the counsellor's judgement as to whether she *ought* to be in possession of additional material to put this specific aim of post-graduate work into a realistic context. He might point out the difficulties involved in obtaining such a post and raise the possibility of widening the range of her aims. Clearly this too might be done in numerous ways. It might trigger the counsellor to embark upon a monologue about the state of the economy and its effect upon post-graduate opportunities in general, it being taken for granted that the captive client needs to know such things. We believe that it should take the form of something like:

'Well Shirley, that's how you may, in principle, do a higher degree in philosophy. In practice though it may not work out so smoothly.'

To which she might declare that she is in fact herself aware of the financial difficulties involved and of the need for a relatively high academic performance from her, when the counsellor might continue with:

'Yes. Being pessimistic for a moment, let's say that it proved impossible for you to get accepted anywhere for one reason or another. Have you any ideas about what to put in its place?'

If, on the other hand, she were to confess her ignorance of the difficulties involved one is likely to arrive at this position of querying the scope of her aim only after explaining the difficulties involved in getting a post-graduate place and money for it.

At the end of any of these, or subsequent stages, she may well, of course, make it clear that she has to, or wants to, go. There is then no justification in insisting that the allotted hour must be filled, so at that point the session will end. Should she be interested the interview could progress in a series of stages aiming ultimately at isolating the set of possibilities that she considers viable enough to warrant her fullest exploration. Whether this is accomplished in this first session, or whether it will require one, or six others is obviously dependent upon the extent to which she has already crystallised realistically her working future, and upon the degree of confidence she has in independently exploiting informational sources available to her. The onus will be upon her to decide at which point in this step-like procedure she opts out of the counselling process; it will be the responsibility of the counsellor, however, to recognise when she has reached this position and to allow her to act upon it without any explicit or implicit contracts, while at the same time making it clear that she is welcome to return at any future time. Thus Shirley might conclude the initial interview with:

'Well, that's given me a lot to think about. I'd better get something sorted out pretty quickly.'

To which the counsellor might respond:

'O.K. Shirley. Let's meet again whenever you feel you want to review things?'

Shirley: Fine. Thanks very much.

Counsellor: Let me show you out.

So much then for our insistence upon a Rogerian approach. In many ways we would maintain that it still is. Obviously in this situation we have been purveying information in a most directive manner, but at the same time preserving always the atmosphere which makes for the client's experience of maximum freedom to be herself within the natural constraints of this type of session.

During an interview of this sort the thoughts of the counsellor are going to be largely focussed upon remembering a set of specific details about a variety of career possibilities, and upon expressing as clearly as possible the appropriate information. Of course, he is again going to be concerned to some extent with such mundane and unbidden ideas as that of the prospect of a cup of coffee, of wondering how he is going to complete some urgent clerical task before the end of the day, of reminding himself that he has to make a phone call at a certain time. He is also going to be potentially alert for cues and signs that indicate that Shirley is wanting to move away from a discussion of her future career to talk, perhaps, about a totally different concern; or he may feel that her perception of career-development is based upon such a distorted stereotype that the direction of the interview might be shifted to examine this topic in some detail.

A COUNSELLING INTERVIEW: 3

The session comprised almost totally of an emotional outburst from a client is relatively rare. When it does occur, especially if it comes after a series of comparatively drama-free interviews, it makes a harsh demand upon the resilience of the counsellor. If he is unable to respond any more constructively than to express 'it can't be as bad as all that', or if he feels so fearful and inadequate that he is too absorbed in trying to restore his own emotional status quo to be able to sustain concentration upon his client's problem, then there is likely to be little value for either client or counsellor in the session. Naturally, a counsellor in this situation (especially if the client is a man) is going to experience an emotional response, and mild anxiety symptoms are going to be generated; he might become aware of increased heart and breathing rates, he might begin to perspire. His thoughts in the initial stages of an interview which has begun by the client bursting into tears and manifesting the deepest despair might well run along the lines of '. . . Oh! God! How can I stop him? What can I say? How can I comfort him? I feel an idiot just watching him. I must *do* something . . .'

In many ways if the client has been a frequent visitor the choice of response is easier. There would be nothing incongruous in expressing concerned surprise—'John! What's happened to you?' With a complete stranger, a similar exclamation might conceivably convey the parallel message 'We're not used to that sort of thing here you know.' So that there is often, at this stage, little value in saying anything. Such a negative decision may be responsible for reducing one dimension of the anxiety the counsellor experiences, for he is released from the pressure of striving to select *le mot juste*.

Doing nothing however, may be effected in a number of ways. One may sit immobile and inscrutable, or with a pained, bored, aloof, exasperated expression upon one's face, none of which is likely to do more than add a fresh dimension of anxiety to the crisis being experienced.

Interest, concern and sympathy may be expressed by the counsellor in both non-verbal and semi-verbal ways, which, assuming the counsellor is a *caring* person, are likely to be manifested spontaneously anyway. Thus, some sort of movement towards the person, some expression of concern, albeit a banal 'Oh! John!' all make for the sort of atmosphere of acceptance that is appropriate. So, perhaps:

John: (weeping bitterly as he slumps into a chair) Oh! God! . . .
Counsellor: John what is it? (Moving his chair close to John's.)
John: (through his tears) . . . No . . . Sorry . . .
Counsellor: O.K. John . . . Try and tell me.
John: . . . Sorry . . . Christ! . . . I've really . . . done it this time . . .
Counsellor: All right John . . .
John: (whose crying seems to have redoubled) . . . Christ! . . . God! . . .
Counsellor: Tell me John . . . it's O.K. . . . (Assuming the two know each other, the counsellor may have some idea as to what could have produced this state) . . . is it about Judy?
John: (Nodding) . . .
Counsellor: Come on John, tell me.

With an unknown client much of the preceding dialogue might well be similar though of course the counsellor is not likely to have any idea of the cause of the outburst. The process might then continue thus:

Mary: . . . it's no good . . .
Counsellor: Here's some more tissues . . . and tell me Mary— please . . .
Mary: . . . I can't . . . I can't . . .
Counsellor: All right, Mary, all right.

In these relatively rare situations where the tears or other manifestations of extreme emotion which prevent articulation occur, the point at which the counsellor has to move from his rôle of comforter is going to depend upon the extent of his knowledge of his client's history, his judgement as to the seriousness of the situation as well as upon the very practical matters of whether his time-table allows him to spend an indefinite time in the rôle, and, on occasions, whether he is easily able to arrange for his client to receive medical attention and, perhaps, admission to a health centre. Assuming that Mary's emotional state appears to be intractable half way through a session, in the middle of a busy day, the counsellor might well adopt a more autocratic rôle while at the same time endeavouring to maintain the security in the relationship that has hopefully been generated. So:

> *Counsellor:* Mary . . . I don't seem to be able to help you . . .
> would you let me take you over to the health centre?
> (Mary just shakes her head) . . . (later) you're *so* unhappy
> Mary, why don't we go and see Dr Smith, there won't
> be any fuss, we'll drive over and go straight up to a room
> . . . come on, let me phone Smithy (Mary sobs 'No!') . . .
> I think we should Mary . . .

If Mary yields to this sort of persuasion the cooperation of the
medical staff must have been taken for granted by the counsellor,
so that she can indeed be admitted without fuss. Of course, Mary
may have continued to resist the pressure in which case the
counsellor must then reorganise his time-table by cancelling
appointments or by having a colleague take over his remaining
clients that day, so that he can be allowed to return to the only
possible rôle of the patient comforter.

Usually, though, there will be a gradual abatement of tears
and a relatively coherent account of the situation will emerge.
From this point on the session is likely to follow the same sort
of pattern as outlined earlier, although the suggestion of utilising
a health centre bed may be gratefully received in order to prevent
the possible embarrassment of having to return to the demands
of the near-communal life of a hall of residence.

OTHER INTERVIEWS

We have so far covered the sort of interview which is relatively
self-contained, with the counsellor content, as it were, with his
ability to handle the difficulties presented within the framework
of 'talking and listening' in a traditional way. In the last illustra-
tion, however, the possibility of utilising another agency was
mentioned. A number of other instances could also have been
cited; for example, arranging a referral to a psychiatrist, arranging
a visit to a professional person in order that the client might gain
some insight into the work and life involved in a career he is
contemplating, or, perhaps, arranging for the assistance of a
member of the teaching staff in a particular sort of study problem.
Where any such external help is deemed appropriate we would
again insist that this can and should be effected in accord with
our general approach. Rather than with a sudden authoritarian
'Ah! you need to see a psychiatrist. I'll just phone him', the
crispness of which might do splendid things for the counsellor's ego, but evoke terror in the client, there seems no reason

why it should not be a matter for discussion, during which the client is free to expose his fears and doubts about, and lack of knowledge of, the implications of a psychiatric consultation.

Apart from such referrals, counselling interviews might well change shape by the introduction of particular, more specialised, techniques of counselling itself. Thus during a second interview, say, by which time the counsellor feels his client can be best helped by the application of a form of behaviour therapy (for example systematic desensitisation), the procedure may radically change from being non-directive and clarificatory into something relatively well-structured and directive; future sessions might involve a combination of both approaches. Again, there need be no sudden disruptive lurch from one to the other so long as the counsellor is willing to introduce the change in such a way that he does not induce alarm or shock, or feelings of rejection, and does not feel the need to express or to imply impatience or exasperation at what has taken place so far. The introduction and administration of behavioural techniques does not, as their critics have been so eager to assert, necessarily and automatically bring the therapeutic relationship spiralling down to an inhuman, mechanistic confrontation. If it does then it is the fault of the counsellor. Similarly there need be no difficulty in introducing the possibility of the client taking a psychological test. Using behaviour therapy as an example the change of direction may be illustrated as follows:

Counsellor: You've explained very fully the sort of feelings you have about examinations, and how they are beginning to colour your whole existence here. I'd like to tell you about an approach to this sort of problem that seems to be pretty successful. It's a technique called 'desensitisation' —you may have heard of it?

Dave: No, I don't think so.

Counsellor: Well, the rationale is that the sort of fears you have experienced have been actually learned by you, as a result of earlier experiences. If this is so the argument is that they can be unlearned. Just as it is a terrifying experience driving a car for the first time, the more you do it the easier it becomes and the more confident you get, and this goes on to the point after which you're hardly conscious of the mechanics of driving, let alone terrified of being on the road. Well desensitisation works on this principle of, sort of, 'getting used to' something; but instead of getting you to go and sit a whole lot of examinations in actuality I would get you to *imagine* them. The other underlying argument is that if you are physically quite relaxed you cannot at the same time feel anxious or tense. All right so far?

Dave: I think so.

Counsellor: So what all this would entail for you would be that first of all I would teach you how to relax, I mean *really* relax, and then working from a list of scenes which we'd sorted out together, I'd tell you to imagine one of them, one which wouldn't worry you much in real life. I'd get you to imagine it for about half a minute, and then go on to the next scene which might be a little more anxiety provoking, and so on until we reach the top of the list. At that point you'd be visualising perhaps the worst sort of examination situation you can think of. The point is, we wouldn't proceed up the list unless you were able to maintain the physical relaxation. If you do all this successfully in imagination then you should find that you can do it in real-life situations without anxiety. Well, that's just a brief outline. Obviously it takes time: exactly how long would depend on how often we could meet, but assuming it was once or twice a week I would think in terms of six months. Well, what's your feeling about all that?

Dave: Well, I don't know really. If you think it'll work . . .

Counsellor: Yes I do, but there can be no absolute guarantees. So I don't want you to feel I'm pressurising you into anything; let's talk a bit more about what is involved and then I'd like you to go away and brood about it all before you come to any decision . . .

Obviously this is a different sort of extract from those previously given, with the counsellor doing almost all the talking, but not in a distant and clinical way, nor in a take-it-or-leave-it fashion. Again by gesture, tone and clear exposition the intention is to convey a basic warmth. The alternative is the 'what-you-need-is . . .' approach followed by a jargon-sprinkled monologue upon the topic, which is less likely to have any real meaning for the bemused and suitably impressed client.

The authority of the counsellor

We have seen something of the variety of situations in which a counsellor may find himself, and we have suggested the range of responses that the counsellor should have at his disposal. Furthermore the basic thinking of the approach has been outlined in earlier chapters. But what of a client's view of such a service? Why does he use it? Why does he continue to use it, and why does he probably recommend that his friends use it? Empirical answers are not easily obtainable and generally seem to be vaguely framed in a because-it-is-there, or, it-seems-to-help response; but what is it that *is* there, that does seems to help? At one level the answer is clear: the Service purveys information crucial to the job-hunter. At the level, however, at which a psychotherapeutic encounter is mutually generated the reasons become speculative. We are convinced that they are inextricably bound up with the concept of authority. Not only 'authority' in the simple sense that the Service's activities are publicly known so that anyone wanting help with a problem will go to the department professionally equipped to deal with it, but also in the sense that those professionals have *credibility* in the way they operate in the intangible field of personal concerns; that what they do is meaningful enough to elicit a client's confidence in, if need be, a continuing therapeutic relationship. This again may seem to be spelling out the obvious, for people are used to taking problems to the relevant professionals. A 'counselling service', however, does not convey the clarity of significance of 'dentist', 'accountant' or 'lawyer', hence confidence is far less readily placed, and will not be at all unless the counsellor merits it. The measure of success in the new profession (in any new profession presumably) lies in the number who voluntarily seek its services.

The onus, then, is upon the counsellor to do, at least adequately, those things he professes to do, and, most important for the present thesis, that he is able and willing to accept the *responsibility* inherent in the counselling relationship. Responsibility, that is, which commits him to his client's well-being and to expending his professional competence through time (not inflexibly in fifty-minute bursts once a week) to ensure that his client is indeed helped as much as is possible. Responsibility, too, which is implicitly recognised and accepted by the client as an ongoing feature of the relationship which he can question and test but upon which he can totally rely for as long as he needs. The extent to which this faith, or confidence, is placed in the counsellor is a measure of his 'authority'. The label 'counsellor' is not sufficient in itself, however worldly-wise or diploma-laden its bearer, to engender the sort of trust a client must be willing to invest in many counselling relationships if they are to have any significant depth or usefulness: the counsellor must primarily have 'authority' before this can happen.

In a time of personal crisis the counsellor may be the only one aware in any comprehensive way of the despair being experienced by a client; despair which casts the counsellor into the rôle of transient protector of an extremely vulnerable and, in many ways, helpless, person: a god-like rôle which may tempt some to believe that whatever they do with a client must be right, for after the event (possibly a disaster for the client) the counsellor can justify any of his actions and ascribe some purpose to explain them. The morality of counselling in our view insists on the awareness of practitioners of their mortality and dictates that they shall not transgress integrity and abuse the 'authority' accorded them, either by exceeding it or, worst of all, by shedding it at a difficult, critical time.

Conclusion

The counselling process, then, may take many forms in a generalist service such as we are advocating. It could be argued that the more forms it does take the better the service, and that versatility is the counsellor's main strength. Basically though the aim remains the same. Whether a counsellor is utilising a behavioural technique, giving vocational information or engaging in a psychodramatic technique the purpose is the clarification of the difficulty which the client is experiencing (whether it be of large or small dimensions) and the attempt to work towards its resolution *with* the client in an atmosphere of friendliness, warmth and understanding.

CHAPTER FIVE

Information problems

Students visiting the premises of the Counselling Service will frequently be in search of information. Indeed, information seeking may well be the most common reason for coming. Certainly it provides the most convenient cover for making contact with the personnel of the service before chancing more highly-charged personal concerns. This means that the counsellors are instinctively alert to the possibility of a client needing more help than simply an answer to the informational query which appears initially to be his sole concern. In this chapter, however, we shall not be dealing with the information seeker who is concealing greater needs. We wish rather to focus attention on the client who comes with a bona-fide informational problem which he wants resolved.

Information and individual needs

Of course, many such clients will never reach the counsellors at all. They will find their questions answered by material that they discover for themselves on the shelves of the Careers Library or, for example, they may find through casual conversation that the secretaries or the administrative assistant are in possession of the relevant knowledge. It is surprising, however, how often students are intimidated by an unfamiliar library or cataloguing system and prefer to come to a counsellor with a question which five minutes of independent research might well have answered for them. Not that we discourage this apparently uneconomic use of our time. On the contrary such an encounter often makes it possible for us to show a student round the Careers Library in a leisurely, informal way and, most important, it enables us to help the student evaluate the information in the context of his own individual needs or ambitions.

It is this emphasis on relating objective information to the particular situation of a given client that characterises our whole approach to this part of our work. Information in a vacuum can be confusing, sometimes even threatening. The student needs the opportunity to incorporate the knowledge he gains into the much broader frame of reference provided by his own feelings about himself and by other situational factors of which he may or may not be aware. This is not to suggest, of course, that we parry direct informational questions or deliberately withhold answers. Such behaviour would show scant respect for the client and might even suggest that we feel we know his needs better than he does. If at all possible, questions are always answered immediately and directly and only then do we proffer the opportunity to evaluate the importance of the information for his own situation. Sometimes, though, questions are not susceptible to such immediate response. It often happens that we do not know the answer although more than likely we do know the appropriate source for extracting the necessary information. In such a case we should not conceal our ignorance but rather explore with the student the possible ways of finding out what he wants. If the information is available in the Careers Library or in other reference works held in the Service we shall more than likely go at once with the student to examine the appropriate material with him on the spot. If, on the other hand, the query involves contacting other people either in the university or elsewhere we shall tell the student who can help him and discuss the next step with him. It is undoubtedly misguided to imagine that all clients want the counsellor to do the work for them. Frequently in situations of this kind the student is not only willing but quite definitely prefers to contact other people himself in order to gain the information he needs. It is tempting for the counsellor to play the part either of the omniscient guru or of the person who has all the right contacts—'I need only pick up the phone'. Such a temptation should sometimes be resisted, for behaviour of this kind, although it may produce the desired information, does not always help the student make the information his own. Here again, the principle at work is the one which stresses the vital importance of relating information to a person's *own* needs and ambitions and this applies as much to the search for information as to the information itself.

STUDENT AND COUNSELLOR INVOLVEMENT

This relating of information to one's own needs is not always a process which can be effected immediately and there is much to be said for at least provisionally fixing a follow-up session for a student if he has received a welter of new information at an initial interview. Again, if a student goes away from a first interview with a pile of literature the least a counsellor can do is to offer the possibility of a further session for reviewing what has been studied. In the event this may prove unnecessary or the student may not desire it but at least the counsellor by his own attitude is indicating to his client that information gathering is an important process which deserves his full attention and involvement. An attitude of mind is then established which may possibly prevent a client at a later date from presenting himself for a job to a recruiting employer without even having bothered to read the job specification.

It must be confessed, though, that it is not always easy for the counsellor himself to maintain this necessary attitude of serious attentiveness to the request for information. The information seeker, if he comes near the end of a long day during which the counsellor has seen three or four clients with complex personal problems, may well be seen as providing a welcome interlude of light relief. If this entails a casual response from the counsellor it may prove disastrous. In the first place he may fail to perceive that the informational enquiry is a mere blind, concealing a greater need but, secondly, even when the enquiry is a perfectly authentic one, he may be tempted to treat it brusquely and automatically or, worst of all, inaccurately.

INACCURATE INFORMATION—A LACK OF RESPECT

It is a frightening thought that inaccurate information may have more serious repercussions for the individual than a badly-handled personal crisis, and yet such is the case. We are only too aware of the unfortunate effect of wrong or inadequate information which students may have obtained from various sources before they reach us at all. Schoolteachers and parents are often the guilty parties and it sometimes turns out that a student has turned his back on a whole range of possible educational and occupational opportunities because he believes that he is insufficiently or inappropriately qualified for them. A recent finalist, for example, believed there was no possibility of his ever becoming a town and country planner because many years before a schoolteacher had informed him, incredibly enough, that only a physics graduate could enter the planning profession. Even more common is the first-year student whose parents have assured him that unless he reads for a science degree he will be unlikely to get a good job at the end of his course—this at a time when there is, for example, an embarrassing surplus of Ph.D. chemists on the job market. An important part of the counsellor's task must be to explode such myths by presenting the facts and by making quite certain that the information he gives or makes available is as reliable and up to date as possible. This is asking a great deal and it is clear that no counselling service can be complete without a staff member—in our case our administrative assistant—whose primary responsibility lies in the informational field. Part of such a person's task must be to service the counsellors by bringing continually to their attention changes, developments and new opportunities as they are announced, for it is virtually impossible for a counsellor with a full case-load to keep himself abreast of all that is going on. What is more, the presence of an informational specialist makes doubly certain that informational counselling is accorded the high priority which it demands. It is no exaggeration to maintain that the way information is handled and presented may be a surer indication of the genuine respect and concern for clients than any other single activity which a counselling service undertakes. It is important to add, however—and this we shall explore at greater length in the chapter on vocational counselling —that information giving, however accurate and up to date, will nearly always be harmful if it comes not as a genuine response to a student's needs or enquiry but as a means of concealing a counsellor's own inability to identify with the real nature of his client's predicament. There is a sense in which a counsellor can arm himself with information in order to keep a troubled client successfully at bay while convincing himself that he is doing a professional and worthwhile job. Nowhere is this danger more likely than in the sphere of vocational counselling.

SOCIAL, PERSONAL INFORMATION

It would be a mistake, however, to imagine that clients seek information only on strictly vocational or academic matters. Increasingly we are finding that questions are brought to us which fall more clearly within the social, personal area. Sometimes clients may want help in interpreting and understanding certain university regulations or in knowing how best to approach local education authorities or admissions officers of other universities. But the area is ever widening. We have been asked to interpret the new abortion law, to comment in general terms on the homosexual stage in human development, to present 'the facts' about cannabis and L.S.D., to explain the procedure for raising a mortgage, to comment on various forms of contraception, and to advise on the disposal of an unwanted car. As with other informational enquiries we respond as directly and objectively as we can to such requests while at the same time making it possible for the client to expose more of his personal situation if he wishes to do so. Usually he does, but sometimes the opportunity is politely but firmly rejected and in such a case we should not dream of pressing the matter. We sometimes feel that by presenting information of this kind in as objective and factual a manner as possible we may appear to some students to be giving the seal of approval to certain activities about which we would, in fact, have many reservations. And yet this seems inevitable if we are to avoid the image of an overtly moralising service which might then repel those very students whose informational queries cloak a more profound value confusion. It is a small price to pay if by allowing a few naïve students to identify us with the vanguard of the permissive society we make it possible for others to seek information as part of an honest attempt to come to terms with their own ethical and social bewilderment. We must confess, however, that as yet we lack the specialist who can assure us that we are fully up to date with all our information in this ill-defined and ever-expanding area of concern. Such a specialisation would certainly not be without its interest!

Initiating information-giving

In this brief chapter we have tried to give some insight into the way we respond to genuine informational enquiries and to stress the vital significance we attach to the handling of information as a whole. It will be noted, however, that we have been concerned here only with information which is given in direct response to a request for it. In later chapters we shall see how it can happen that a skilled counsellor will himself sometimes initiate information-giving as a means of aiding the counselling process. But when this happens there is no less need for information which is complete, accurate and up to date, nor is there any relaxation of the principle that information is valuable only in so far as it is carefully and purposefully related to the client's own situation, needs, abilities and perceptions of himself.

CHAPTER SIX

Vocational exploration

It is common practice to isolate vocational counselling from the rest of the counselling operation. In British universities the usual model is that of the Appointments Service or Careers Advisory Service staffed by 'officers' or 'advisers' whose concern is entirely with vocational matters. These services, although they are often attempting an impossibly difficult task with great dedication, are not, on the whole, held in high esteem by the student population. Frequently they are criticised on the score that they provide excellent information for those students who have already decided what they want to do but offer little help to the confused and uncertain individual who is a long way from making realistic vocational decisions. Usually they are woefully understaffed with the result that in some instances the waiting list for interviews can extend over several weeks.

It is our contention, as we have stated earlier, that vocational counselling should not be hived off in this way into a separate, specialist department. It makes more sense, in our view, to see vocational decision-making as a vital strand in the overall development of a young person. Vocational counselling, therefore, is not merely concerned with the provision of information nor even with the exploration of aptitudes and interests. It is concerned rather with the whole person as he seeks to come to an understanding of himself, his values and his aims. Clearly in some cases a lengthy process can be involved which underlines even more emphatically the inadequacy of a service which can do little more than offer the individual student a single interview during his final year at the university.

This is not to suggest, however, that students can be induced to consider vocational planning before they feel motivated to do so. Many an appointments service has tried to approach students early on in their undergraduate careers but often there has been little return for its effort. The reason is clear. When students first arrive at a university they are not, with some exceptions, inclined to project three or four years into the future. They are more concerned with the immediate problems of academic study and social adjustment. To most of them, therefore, an appointments service seems at best an irrelevance and at worst an unwarranted intrusion. The same cannot be said of a general counselling service which is seen to be responding to the immediate needs of individuals as they experience them. It frequently happens that the first hint of vocational significance arises in the context of something seemingly far removed from such considerations—the student attempting to cope with a neurotic friend, for example, begins dimly to perceive himself as a 'helping' person or for another the need to pay off a large overdraft focusses attention, perhaps for the first time, on the connection between life-style and income. It is unlikely in such a situation that the counsellor would spell out the point and yet the learning takes place all the same through the counselling process. If the student subsequently returns to the same counsellor with a directly expressed vocational concern there will already be some basis of knowledge and shared experience on which to build.

Confusion in the final year

Despite the contact we have with many students from all years, for a host of different reasons, it nevertheless often happens that some approach us for the first time as they near the end of their undergraduate career. Such clients are often in a state of great vocational confusion and uncertainty. Their expectations of us at this point vary enormously. Some believe that we shall be annoyed with them for being so undecided while others expect us to settle the whole issue for them by telling them what to do at the end of a thirty-minute interview. Needless to say both these groups would be well wide of the mark in their expectations.

The traditional response would probably take the form of a gentle but determined questioning session during which the interviewer would attempt to assess the student in terms of his educational qualifications and interests. This in turn would be followed by a knowledgeable exposition of the various rôles which the student might care to explore more fully. This model of vocational counselling leaves the initiative very much with the counsellor. It is he who poses the questions and he who suggests possible answers. The method is very much akin to that of the diagnostician who determines the nature of an illness and then prescribes a possible remedy. We feel that such an approach often fails to involve the client fully and leaves him vaguely dissatisfied. The dissatisfaction can be acute when the client goes away with the uncomfortable feeling that the counsellor has analysed him, labelled him and decreed him accountant or bank clerk or Royal Army Pay Corps—without at any point relating to him at anything beyond a superficial level. Nevertheless this method is still universally practised and when very little time is available it is perhaps churlish to be too critical of those who employ it. It would be dishonest to pretend that we never fall into such behaviour ourselves but at least we know that, when we do so, we are running contrary to the principles we profess.

It is indisputable, however, that the traditional approach fails to take proper account of two fundamental ideas which recur repeatedly in the literature of vocational development theory—the idea of the self-concept and the notion that vocational maturity is the outcome of a number of growth stages. Both these ideas imply a high regard for the individual's uniqueness and a sensitivity to his readiness or unreadiness for decision-making. They also require of the client a preparedness to undergo a fairly rigorous process of self-exploration.

Self-exploration

Self-exploration is not a process which is immediately acceptable to all students. The encouragement to begin on such an undertaking is resented by some who see it as a somewhat impertinent trespassing into their private concerns. The possibility of such resistence must be recognised at the outset but at the same time the counsellor needs to be aware of the novelty of the task for many of his clients. It is an astonishing and disturbing fact that the educational experience of many young people has at no point, apparently, required them to take stock of themselves. They have been at the receiving end of a process which has fed them with more and more knowledge but which has not equipped them in any way for the pursuit of self-knowledge. In some cases it would seem that the necessity for vocational decision-making presents perhaps the final opportunity for a conscious exploration of the self.

Those who are prone to much introspection and self-analysis do not always appreciate the fear which is generated in many people by the task of self-exploration. At root the fear is of discovering nothing or of unearthing feelings which then become uncontrollable or profoundly disturbing. It is such a fear which each year keeps many students firmly away from the clutches of careers advisers. For such people the risk is too great. Self-exploration, they dimly suspect, may lead to the shattering realisation that they have no real interests, no proven capabilities and consequently no chance of an acceptable rôle in society.

For others there is a fear of a different order. These are the students who have looked long and hard at our society and have decided, rightly or wrongly, that they want no part of it. Such students are often among the most intelligent and frequently they will have been in the forefront of political activity during their time in the university. The intensity of the feelings which they often experience is seldom appreciated by those whose business it is to help them plan for the future, and yet for them the predicament can be agonisingly acute. While they are students it is not difficult for them to criticise and snipe at society from the comparative security and safety of an academic institution. The moment of graduation, however, sees the end of such security. The situation takes on an altogether more sinister aspect. The student is faced by what must seem the acid test of his authenticity and integrity. To opt in may be viewed both by him and by his close associates as an act of treachery—a cowardly compromise in the face of economic necessity or powerful external pressures, perhaps, from troubled parents or advisers. To opt out, on the other hand, needs great courage and can be viewed as mere escapism or a total retreat from reality. In short, there occurs at this point a crisis which strikes at the very heart of such a student's intellectual and emotional life.

FALSE EXPECTATIONS OF THE COUNSELLOR

The fear of facing personal inadequacy and the fear of undergoing a crisis of values are both widespread in the student population and both, we feel, constitute major obstacles to the process of self-exploration. They also have important implications for the way in which vocational counselling is offered in the university setting. It is clear, for instance, that considerable energy must be devoted to the destruction of preconceived ideas and expectations which many students still have of 'careers advisers'. It is not easy to summarise these coherently but they include the following misconceptions:

1. Careers advisers expect you to know what you want to do before you come to them. They merely provide information.
2. Careers advisers are out to get you a job whether you want it or not.
3. Careers advisers know all about industry and commerce and are by implication upholders of the capitalist system. They are allied with employers and act largely as their agents.
4. Careers advisers are not interested in feelings and values. They are concerned with aptitudes and opportunities.
5. Careers advisers do not give clients more than one or two interviews.
6. Careers advisers are walking encyclopaedias or ought to be.

At Keele we do our best to counter such misconceptions through our literature and through letters to individual students which stress our willingness to help no matter what stage a student may be at in his vocational thinking. Our weekly bulletins about employment opportunities and post-graduate courses and the range of the careers talks and seminars which we convene also indicate clearly that we are interested in all types of work and hold no special brief for industry, the Civil Service or any other area of employment. Despite these very conscious efforts, however, we are convinced that we would do little to allay the anxieties of some of our potential clients if it were not for the fact that we are known to be operating a general counselling service and cannot therefore be seen as part of a wicked capitalist plot.

It is one thing, however, to be aware of the fears and obstacles operating against self-exploration but quite another to know how to cope with these when they present themselves in the person of an individual client on a wet afternoon in the autumn term. Most frequently such a client will not fall into either of the two extreme categories that we have already described. More likely

D

our client will be an average, coping student who has come along 'to talk about careers'. It is probable that he will have only a vague notion of the way the counsellor is likely to respond to him. It is equally probable, however, that somewhere in the back of his mind will be the expectation that the counsellor will somehow present him with a range of possible jobs and advise him which one to aim for. Furthermore he may well expect the whole procedure to be completed in the space of a forty-five minute interview.

THE COUNSELLING 'CONTRACT'

In the light of these confused expectations we often feel it incumbent upon us to define the nature of the help we are offering at the outset. It is perhaps not too wide of the mark to suggest that we are outlining a form of contract by which the counselling relationship will be defined and regulated and it is up to the student to determine whether or not the contract is acceptable to him before we proceed further. The point is perhaps best made by citing verbatim the kind of exchange which often takes place at the beginning of such an encounter.

Counsellor: Well, how can I be of help to you?

Student: Well, I thought it was about time I came along to chat about careers, you know. I've had a few vague ideas but I don't really know what I want to do.

Counsellor: You feel it's a question of starting from scratch?

Student: Almost, I reckon. You know, I feel there's so few jobs I know anything about.

Counsellor: And perhaps if you knew more you'd find something that really suited you.

Student: Well, it's possible, I suppose. Anyway, I've got to do something about it haven't I?

Counsellor: Mm.

Student: A lot of my friends have been along to you and I suppose it's catching. And anyway I don't want to be one of the great unemployed next year.

Counsellor: Which means you're pretty anxious to start getting things sorted out now before finals start creeping up on you.

Student: Yes, and I don't really know how to set about it.

Counsellor: Well, we'll certainly do our best to help you get started. Before we go any further, though, I think it might

be worthwhile saying one or two things about the whole
process of career choice. If you think about it, it's obviously pretty absurd to imagine that the answer can be
pulled out of a hat like magic. Nor am I going to be in a
position to tell you what to do by the end of today's
session, for instance—nor am I ever likely to do that if
I'm honest.

Student: Oh!

Counsellor: The point I'm trying to make is that we've
probably got quite a process ahead of us and that it will
need some working at. What's more it's not much use
my trotting out a lot of information about possible jobs
unless I know a great deal more than I do at the moment
about you. So that's where we've got to start really—
with you and the sort of person you feel you are and the
sort of satisfactions you would hope to look for in any
job you take up. How do you feel about approaching it
like that?

Student: Yeah—O.K. Bit difficult, though, isn't it? I mean,
I've never really thought about myself like that. I'm not
sure I know what sort of person I am really. What do you
mean exactly?

Counsellor: Well, there are several ways of trying to look at
it. For instance, we could begin by attempting to see you
through the eyes of some of your friends. How do you
imagine they think about you—and how accurate are they
in their assessments? Do you think that might be a possible
way?

Student: That makes me think, I must say. I'll have a go,
though, if you like.

Such a client is clearly beginning to respond to the approach
which the counsellor is advocating. He is expressing a kind of
willingness to accept the contract which the counsellor is offering,
although at this stage he cannot know fully what is entailed.
There is no doubt that the counsellor is directing the course of
the session but he is doing so out of respect for the client and his
needs. Nothing is worse than colluding with false expectations
and there is always the danger that this will occur if the counsellor does not spell out the kind of task which faces the client
and the nature of the help which he as a professional is able to
offer. A contract of this kind, by defining and clarifying the

relationship, does not trespass upon the client's freedom of action but offers him on the contrary the kind of context in which he can begin to explore himself purposefully and without embarrassment.

Difficulties in self-exploration

The elimination of embarrassment is important. Those who are unaccustomed to talking about themselves frequently fall victim to a form of inhibition which prevents them from embarking upon what, in other circumstances, they would regard as mildly improper self-revelation. The effect of defining the task and suggesting the method of approach is to remove much of this embarrassment and to replace it by a sense of purpose which is actually strengthened by the process of self-exploration itself. Not that the process is always an easy one. On the contrary for some it seems painfully slow and difficult and no matter how skilled the counsellor is there can occur the kind of impasse which seems to render further progress well-nigh impossible. In such cases both counsellor and client can experience a frustration which is potentially very damaging, for it can make the counsellor feel totally incompetent and the client unresponsive and uncooperative. In every case the situation must be acknowledged and confronted for frustration breeds depression and depression can lead to a sense of hopelessness about the whole enterprise. For the counsellor to discontinue at this point may well induce in the client the feeling that after all his future must be left in the hands of fate. What follows is an attempt to present directly the various ways in which such encounters might occur and develop.

DIFFICULT CLIENT: I

> *Counsellor:* And you feel somehow you're not that sort of person?
> *Student:* I dunno, really.
> *Counsellor:* That's the sort of situation where you don't really know how to respond at all.
> *Student:* Yes.
>   Silence.
> *Counsellor:* It seems to me we've come up against something of a brick wall and don't know how to deal with it. Do you feel that too?

Student: Well, it's all pretty pointless isn't it?

Counsellor: How do you mean?

Student: Well, you go on doing your best to get me to talk. But you know and I know that the truth of the matter is that I don't really want a job at all.

Counsellor: That the whole business is something you'd rather not be involved in.

Student: Yes, because I just can't see how there *can* be any sort of job which I'd enjoy.

In this interview the counsellor, by confronting the apparent impasse, has enabled the client to voice his fundamental anxiety. The student feels that the whole undertaking is doomed from the outset because in his view, no rôle can possibly exist which would bring him satisfaction. Once this fear has been openly expressed, however, it is likely that a whole area of confusion will be revealed. Such students—and they seem increasingly common—are not among the radical critics of society nor do they necessarily hold strong political views. Frequently they are the most gentle of people and the likelihood is that they have enjoyed their time at the university and made good satisfactory relationships. In a sense their education has been almost too pleasurable with the result that they cannot conceive of a more desirable experience. Anything must be a change for the worse. If they are able students such people will almost invariably think at some stage of doing post-graduate work with the mistaken idea that this will ensure a continuation of their present mode of living. If they are not particularly able and this escape route is barred to them the problem often becomes immediate and acute. The very mention of the word 'career' is enough to send shivers down their spines for it seems to imply a fixed and inevitable route towards a determined and probably distant goal. There is also the prospect of 'training programmes', of pecking orders and ambitious colleagues bent on quick promotion. For a student who has learnt to regulate his own life, to attach importance to openness and flexibility and to value other people such a prospect must be at best daunting, at worst annihilating. He begins to feel that the world has no place for a person with his values and his apparently simple needs. There is nothing for it but to go on the dole or join a commune.

Such feelings of hopelessness spring from the experience of a way of life, the implications of which have never been fully examined, and from a sometimes astonishing ignorance of the opportunities available. It is unlikely therefore that the counsellor will be of use to such a client unless he is prepared to confront the mounting resistance and depression which the attempt at self-exploration quickly engenders.

DIFFICULT CLIENT: 2

In other instances self-exploration can prove difficult for quite different reasons.

> *Counsellor:* And when you think about your friends it's difficult to know how they see you?
> *Student:* Yes, I've never really thought about it, to be honest.
> *Counsellor:* It's very strange to you this business of self-appraisal.
> *Student:* Yes—I feel a right idiot, really. I don't seem to know anything about myself do I?
> *Counsellor:* It may be that you've never had the opportunity to do this sort of thing before—or never felt the need.
> *Student:* Yes, that's it. I've just drifted along, I suppose, without being very conscious of anything.
> *Counsellor:* And yet now you feel you would like to open it up a bit?
> *Student:* Oh, yes, sure. I see the point but I just don't seem able to begin.
> *Counsellor:* Often in such a situation people in the past have found it helpful to take one of our interest tests—just to get started, as it were. How would you feel about that?
> *Student:* Sounds interesting—and you think it could be of some help?
> *Counsellor:* Yes, I do. Mind you, we treat these tests with caution but I do feel they can be genuinely helpful to someone like yourself who finds it difficult to sort out his thoughts in cold blood.
> *Student:* O.K. then. How do I do this test?

The use of tests

We are aware that the word 'test' is technically inappropriate to describe measures of 'interest', but it has become so much a part of the vernacular that we continue to use it.

INTEREST TESTS

The client in the case we have just described is a man who is genuinely concerned to fulfil his part of the contract as the counsellor has presented it to him. He wishes to look at himself in a conscious and constructive way and yet the process is so alien to his previous mode of thought and behaviour that he finds it almost impossibly difficult to cooperate. In such a situation it has in our experience often proved constructive to encourage the student to take a vocational interest test. For him the test then becomes a way of analysing and expressing his feelings and needs. The stimulus of the questions upon which he can reflect in solitude enables him to embark painlessly upon a task which was previously difficult or even frightening. The mere discovery that it is possible to make choices is also reassuring and frequently the client returning for a test interpretation is already more confident and more involved in the decision-making process simply as a result of having taken the test and finding that he can respond to it. What is more, the test result provides both the counsellor and the client with common material which can serve as a point of departure for the kind of exploration which previously seemed almost impossible.

Interest tests are by no means the answer to every difficulty nor are they the instant remedy for every recalcitrant client. Used indiscriminately they can be positively harmful, for they may give the client the impression that he is simply being 'processed' in a way which, far from strengthening his confidence, will tend to reduce the counsellor in his eyes to the rank of a psychological technician of doubtful usefulness. Nevertheless we are convinced that for the right client at the right time such tests have a real and positive value and strengthen rather than weaken the counselling relationship. It goes without saying that the way the test is presented and the way in which the interpretation is subsequently handled are always of crucial importance. Clients are only too prone to see in a test result either what they want to see or what they fear to see. It requires every ounce of the counsellor's skill to ensure that they understand what the result actually is saying without taking away with them implications which the test could not possibly support. Counsellors untrained in the use and interpretation of tests are very unlikely to avoid such pitfalls and would be wise to exercise the utmost caution in the use of test material however simple and straightforward the test might superficially appear.

APTITUDE TESTS

To some it may seem surprising that interest tests have been discussed without, as yet, any mention of tests of aptitude. Surely, it could be argued, knowing a person's interests is of little value without some knowledge of his capabilities. In fact, however, with the notable exception of a computer aptitude test, we find ourselves using such tests only on rare occasions. Such an occasion might arise when a student's interests seem on the face of it to run almost counter to what one might expect from his previous academic training and background. In most cases, however, the available tests are not sufficiently discriminating at this level and with this kind of population to prove particularly helpful. Their chief value lies in their capacity to reassure the occasional student who has produced an unexpected interest profile that it is not being altogether unrealistic to pursue what might otherwise seem a very fanciful line of thought. Certainly this has been a striking outcome of the computer aptitude test, the results of which have persuaded many an arts student to consider the computer field with the utmost seriousness. At the risk of generalising overmuch, however, it seems likely that at university level a student's marked interest in a specific area of activity indicates at least the potential ability to master that activity.

TESTS OF THE FUTURE?

Recently we have begun to feel that the task of self-exploration would be greatly helped forward in many cases by tests which could throw more light on motivational factors and questions of value. It can happen, for example, that both interest and aptitude tests *seem* to be indicating a possible financial career but this will be to little purpose if the student concerned sees no value in financial undertakings and cannot anyway arouse enough energy even to explore such opportunities. 'I suppose I ought to want to bother but I don't' is a common enough response and tests which could in some way help to penetrate the inertia would prove invaluable. As yet our experience does not permit us to do more than express the pious hope that instruments will be developed which will prove helpful in this area.

A job is a way of life

It is probably true to say that a basic assumption underlying all our work in vocational counselling is that a job is more than a job—it is a life-style, something which conditions not only what we earn, but also the circle of our friends and acquaintances, the nature of our leisure, the sense of fulfilment we are likely to experience as individual human beings. Because of this basic assumption, however, we can sometimes find ourselves in deep water.

DIFFICULT CLIENT: 3

> *Student:* You seem to be treating this whole business very seriously.
> *Counsellor:* I suppose I am: that's the way it strikes me.
> *Student:* Anybody would think that the job you did determined the sort of person you are.
> *Counsellor:* Perhaps there is a certain amount of truth in that —although I would prefer to say that the sort of person you want to become will determine the kind of job you will find satisfying.
> *Student:* You really are hung up on this work thing, aren't you? I couldn't care less what I do as long as it brings me in some bread and doesn't send me completely round the bend. You just tell me what I *could* do and leave the rest to me. I'm prepared to be anything from a park-keeper to a long-distance lorry-driver if you reckon I'd be taken on.

With students such as this we do well to be especially aware of the primary task of helping them to understand themselves and not to be merely concerned with their making 'good' choices. In most cases we shall be right in assuming that the selection of the occupational rôle will be of great importance in the life of the individual but in a few cases it may well be relatively inconsequential. Clearly it would be wrong to accept the statement of this last-quoted client completely at its face value—much could be lurking behind it. The student could, for example, be cloaking a reluctance to accept responsibility for himself or concealing a deep-seated sense of inferiority. After exploration, however, it might emerge that he was indeed a person who was able to establish a sense of purpose and self-esteem without reference to

his work rôle. Such people do exist and usually they are among
the most self-aware. It would be impertinent of a counsellor to
seek to undermine such a stance. His task would be to help the
client discover a job which could be integrated most readily into
the pattern of the other activities which were of primary significance to him. A passionate painter of seascapes, for example,
might well be happier teaching in a south coast language school
than engaging in market research in Manchester.

VOCATIONAL IMMATURITY

It is increasingly common to find students who quickly admit
to their own immaturity and almost plead to be released from
the task of vocational decision making at the point of graduation.
These students differ from the 'there can't be any job I could
enjoy' group insofar as they have by no means always found
their university career a pleasurable experience nor have they
achieved the degree of personal autonomy which often characterises the other group. Frequently, however, they have a very
clear understanding of their own needs.

DIFFICULT CLIENT: 4

> *Student:* I don't feel I'm in any position to know what I want
> to do. I've been in education without a break since I was
> four and I just feel I want a breathing space for a while
> before committing myself to anything.
> *Counsellor:* You feel you've become a bit institutionalised
> yourself.
> *Student:* Yes, I do. It's all so easy isn't it? Food and shelter
> provided, entertainment laid on, lectures to attend—all
> neatly there to be gobbled up.
> *Counsellor:* And in the process not much chance to find out
> what you really want.
> *Student:* I've never bothered. The university thing often seems
> pretty boring and pointless but I suppose I'll stagger
> through to the end now. I just feel I need to grow up a
> bit, stand on my own feet for a while before committing
> myself.

The need is clearly stated but the ways of remedying it are
by no means always evident. The student who expresses himself
in this fashion may often be concealing a host of personal anxieties
and inadequacies and these have to be revealed before his desire

for personal growth can be realistically explored. It sometimes happens that the counselling process itself does much to confer a sense of adulthood on the student and often, once the feeling of immaturity has been examined thoroughly, possible courses of action begin to suggest themselves. In some cases it becomes clear that the student is experiencing no more than a natural apprehension at the approach of a new stage in life and all that is required is the reassurance that decisions taken at this point are not irreversible. Again, the student who feels he has never really escaped from the parental clutches may come to see that committing himself to steady employment may be the best possible way of asserting his independence as a separate entity from the family.

For some there are peculiarly contemporary difficulties raised by the changing attitudes in our society to the sex rôles. Girls are frequently uncertain about what they want of themselves as women. It is difficult, for example, for the girl who feels that her main ambition is to marry and have children to reconcile this with the needs she feels she ought to have (and which others manifestly do have) as a person of high intellectual ability. Men, too, are frequently perturbed by the need they experience to provide nurturance or to express affection and wonder if their attraction to teaching or social work is merely a sign of sexual abnormality. These students and others like them have a genuine need for experience and situations which will not only provide the opportunity for testing themselves in new ways but also the time for the self-appraisal and reflection of which they have previously deprived themselves or been deprived. Such young people often present their need in terms of a desire to travel and one cannot help feeling that the journey they are really seeking is inwards rather than to distant lands. A year abroad teaching English to foreign students often seems, in a most satisfying manner, to provide travelling experience in both dimensions: 'I went to Casablanca and found myself'!

The exploratory stage

This last group serves as a powerful reminder that few students will have advanced beyond the exploratory stage in their vocational development. Many will only now be at the beginning of that stage and will be experiencing the feelings which circumstances forced on many of their less intellectually gifted contemporaries four or even seven years previously. Even those who have followed specifically vocational courses—social workers, teachers, engineers, even doctors—may well, as the moment of 'being qualified' approaches, experience profound and disturbing doubts and misgivings. For others on vocational courses the uncertainties may come much earlier—even in the first term. In either case the sense of being trapped, of being processed into a mould which is no longer acceptable, can be overwhelming. Such conflicts need to be faced. Confronting doubts often leads to their resolution and the feeling that, after all, the career choice is an acceptable one. Where this does not prove to be the case the courage to accept that a mistake has been made is the necessary prelude to a more appropriate choice. It is in this kind of situation that students who do not have access to a professional counsellor or an outside agent may find themselves in considerable difficulty. Students in a college of education, for example, may find it almost impossible to voice their doubts to tutors who, they feel, will try to offer false reassurance about a profession in which they have a vested interest. Similarly an engineering student in a large technological institution may be appalled at the thought of confessing to his tutor that he would prefer to be reading English Literature.

VOCATIONAL DEVELOPMENT AND THE IMPLICATIONS FOR EDUCATION
AND COUNSELLING

The realisation that the exploratory stage of vocational development might well be expected to persist quite naturally into the mid-twenties or even later has important implications for educators in general and counsellors in particular. For educators the obvious message is the danger of academic over-specialisation at a premature stage. It is clearly desirable that as many doors as possible should be left open for as long as possible so that the range of opportunities available to the developing person is not limited to posts requiring his particular specialism or expertise. Courses of study not only condition what is actually studied. They can also have a telling effect on a student's attitudes and here again a narrow specialist course is hardly likely to foster the flexibility which is required if vocational exploration is to be encouraged. What is more it is becoming increasingly clear that our society is evolving in such a way that the need for specialists is greatly outweighed by the demand for flexible generalists who have so secure a sense of identity that they are capable, both educationally and attitudinally, of equipping themselves for new rôles and learning new skills in a rapidly changing world.

The counsellor needs to be the enemy of fixed attitudes and blinkered thinking. He needs to explode the myth of the 'safe profession', the virtue of the strictly vocational course, the superiority of science over the rest. Instead he needs to campaign for courses which allow people to shift in their vocational aims or discover them for the first time without feeling that they have thereby invalidated their present course of study but rather that the learning experience itself is part-agent in their personal and vocational development. He needs, too, to encourage students— possibly through small group discussion—to sample various aspects of the world of work in a purposeful way during their vacations. In this connection he must seek to persuade employers of all kinds that they would be rendering an invaluable service by making such opportunities available to students, especially during the summer months. Clearly he will not be in a position to do this unless he himself is constantly visiting employers and exploring both conventional and unconventional work settings.

When all this has been achieved, however, the counsellor may be sure that many, if not most, of his clients will turn their backs on the opportunities for vocational exploration which he has sought to create for them. He must be patient and not complain too bitterly when the vocational confusion that he feels could have been tackled slowly and methodically two years previously is presented as a crisis in the final year or even on the final day. It is, after all, from the individual's response to crisis that growth arises and the counsellor's task is to ensure that he aids the individual in a way which will facilitate that growth. A crisis has the merit of being taken seriously by the person undergoing it. The counsellor will fail if his behaviour betrays neither an appreciation of the crisis nor an ability to work constructively from the starting point which it provides. 'If only you had come sooner' is the cry of a doctor who is about to read his patient the death sentence before prescribing a palliative of despair.

Finding out about the job

It would be incorrect to imagine that all students find the task of self-exploration difficult or threatening. On the contrary for

many it is both a pleasurable and relatively straightforward undertaking. Often they will have largely accomplished the task before
coming to the counsellor and need only to hear themselves
speaking their thoughts aloud to be reinforced and reassured in
their own self assessment and sense of identity. The problem is
then no longer who am I but, quite simply, what job am I going
to do?

The counsellor, if he has been able to identify satisfactorily
with his client, should at this point be in a position to provide
information to which the client can respond spontaneously. If
self-exploration has genuinely taken place, and if the results have
been expressed by the client in his own words and *not in the form
of answers to questions which the counsellor has pre-ordained* the
ground is ready for the sowing of occupational ideas. In some
cases the counsellor must wait a long time before this moment
arrives and with certain clients it may not arrive at all. The
timing is crucial. The counsellor who steps in clumsily and too
soon must inevitably lose the confidence of his client, for he is
demonstrating a lack of understanding springing from an unwillingness to wait until the point is reached when there is
sufficient insight on his part to move in sensitively with the
specific information. Information giving when it takes place in
this way in the context of vocational exploration presents its own
problems.

It is not difficult to obtain factual knowledge of a certain
kind about most occupations. The literature now available is often
detailed and reliable as far as it goes. The job insofar as it takes
the form of a particular activity or activities may well be described fully and accurately and there will almost certainly be a
detailed discussion of training, salaries and prospects. Such information, however, despite its superficial completeness, by no
means tells the whole story. It dwells on the materialistic and
technical aspects of jobs but it does little or nothing to illuminate
the psycho-social factors involved in any occupation. It is precisely in this area that the counsellor needs to exercise all the
professional skill he can muster. If his research into different
careers has enabled him to quote statistics and to give detailed
job descriptions with a shrewd analysis of long-term prospects
he will provide his clients with no more than a good manual or
a well-produced employer's hand-out. If on the other hand he
is concerned to explore what *it feels like* to be a solicitor or a

bank manager and to identify imaginatively not only with the professional rôle but also with the social rôle and the personal life-style of various occupations he may be in a position to guide his client into an area of occupational information which is seldom covered in the books and which, in any case, demands a knowledge of the individual if it is to be transmitted in a helpful way. This is demanding a great deal of the counsellor, and in many cases he may be able to do little more than work imaginatively with the more or less stereotyped impression that he has of a given occupation. Nevertheless his emphasis on the factors which seldom find a place in the conventional careers literature will serve to alert the student to a whole area of consideration which he might otherwise neglect or not even take into account.

If self-exploration has been accomplished successfully, counsellor and client will share an understanding not only of the client's interests and potential abilities but also of his need for achievement, his need for relationship, his feelings about authority and organisation, his desire for status and material possessions, the nature of his ethical and philosophical beliefs, even perhaps, his need for such physical things as the sea or the city. It is in the light of his understanding of factors such as these that the counsellor dares to offer suggestions and information. In this way the information is 'personalised' and it is offered not as cold fact but as a global and in many ways subjective impression which attempts to incorporate the intangible qualities concerned with feeling and value.

Not that any counsellor worth his salt would be content to leave it there. However wide his experience and however well-developed his ability to identify imaginatively he cannot hope to do more than give tentative indications of what it feels like to be leading the life of a stockbroker or that of an unattached female social worker. He will be anxious for his client to meet and talk with the 'real thing' and to this end, within the bounds of practicability, he will do his best to bring about such confrontations whenever possible. In a way the whole process is concerned with reality testing. The criticism which can be directed against much that has passed for vocational counselling in the past is that counsellors have been concerned with a very incomplete reality. Of course salaries, prospects and job descriptions are important but they are only a small part of the reality which is made up of all the implications of the total life-style of an occupational rôle. It is our belief that it is with this larger reality that the vocational counselling process is ultimately concerned. Perhaps this is why we are so frequently dissatisfied with what we feel we achieve. The task, after all, is formidable.

CHAPTER SEVEN

Academic concerns

Academic concerns may be defined here as those difficulties which hinder the successful technical pursuance of a course of study. They arise either from a pure inability to cope with academic demands or from a change in personal circumstances which militates against sustaining technical competence. This chapter will not be concerned with an exploration of how such underlying problems as the latter may be interpreted and alleviated as this is the province of chapter eight. Here we shall be looking at the form such referrals may take and the ways in which the symptoms may be tackled.

To some the need to write a chapter in a book such as this on 'academic concerns' would be a mystery. For many, in Britain anyway, the logic is simple: all the bright people ('bright' because they have all had to pass stringent examinations), leave school and go into universities or into higher education of some sort; they have the intellectual equipment to cope with such advanced work, therefore there is no reason to suppose that they might fail on intellectual grounds, and therefore there is no reason why they should fail at all. The other frequently expressed view reverses this—that failure in higher education is *only* justifiable when it turns out that Johnny is not bright enough. Both views only take accounts of bits of people, rather than their indisputable wholeness. Although we seem to be doing the same by chopping up counselling referrals into 'vocational', 'academic' and 'personal' problems, it is hoped that it will be seen to be necessary for the sake of clarity. In fact, even within this one category of problems, it will be apparent that there are many individual differences in the presenting symptoms, and that difficulties are complex and interrelated.

A general view

It is clear to most who work in higher education that the process of extended study with its many points at which individuals are assessed and graded, and with its final crescendo of examinations, does create unique stresses for its participants. Students, as human beings, are going to react to such stresses in numerous ways and with varying degrees of intensity: to expect otherwise is to have a utopian view of human psychology. In fact, intellectual ability *per se* is likely to have very little to do with academic failure or decisions to leave the institution once a person is at university.

'Academic concerns', then, fall naturally into two main types. Firstly, those that have a basis in a real, difficult, situation. The person has had bad marks in written work or in examinations, for example. Secondly, those that are imagined or presumed because events have not yet substantiated them; thus, the person who feels that he is doomed to failure as he does not seem to have read as much as everyone else and does not see how he can pass imminent exams. It is proposed to treat each of these separately, but first it will be useful to look at some facets of counselling that are common to each, and some counselling activities that feature rather more prominently in dealing with this range of difficulties than in others.

This is the area in which the counsellor can have most contact with academic and administrative colleagues, whether it is to discover the reality of a student's thinking by having certain regulations interpreted by the institution's expert, or whether it is to find out precisely what a student's academic standing is within a department, or whether it is to negotiate for some modified or special tuition with a member of the teaching staff. Such activities often call for diplomatic handling if confidentiality is to be preserved in those cases where the student understandably cannot summon up the sort of courage required to identify his 'weaknesses' to those responsible for assessing him academically.

The presentation of 'academic concerns' does not seem to be confined to any stage in progress through a course of study (though the specific area of 'subject choice' can only be raised *before* a particular point after which decisions are irrevocable), nor is it restricted by sex or age, nor by discipline, nor, indeed, does it always appear to be by personality, or by circumstances or by institution. Such problems reflect the inevitable occupational hazards of being a student. There are naturally varying degrees of intensity with which individuals are burdened by such concerns, but in general these really *are* the 'normal' problems of 'normal' people undergoing prolonged study, which may arise at any time.

The counsellor's work within this area is likely to entail his being active in a number of rôles—that of the negotiator who phones or meets with key people on a client's behalf, or of the director/experimenter who engages with the client in problem-solving behaviour. For it is here that the counsellor can quickly obtain concrete feed-back—he *did* get the essay written after all, he *did* find it impossible to remain for longer than half an hour in Friday's tutorial, she was *not* able to sit that particular examination, and so on. Such activity has also special implications for client contact and the pacing of the therapeutic endeavour, for in many cases it seems relevant to meet frequently and briefly over a short period of time, though where the overlap into the 'personal problem' area is extensive, such a generalisation becomes patently false. In working with this kind of problem, too, the counsellor becomes more aware of his rôle as an educator. Whether or not the teachers themselves could, or should, have the responsi-bility for identifying and coping with what, after all, are some-times basic learning difficulties is hardly a useful question when a steady stream of sufferers, some of whom have not had help from this quarter and some who do not want such help, pass through a non-academic, non-teaching counselling department. One can only wonder wryly and ironically why an institution devoted to learning has no provision to teach the skills of learning; why it seems to be tacitly assumed that all its members will all the time manifest such skills; why the specialist departments of education and psychology fail to recognise either the need or the possibility for training in the acquisition or polishing of such skills.

The problems: 1

The first sub-category will be filled by those 'concerns' which have a basis in reality at any given time, in events that *are* happen-ing or *have* happened. The list is long as it includes:

1. those who have failed exams;
2. those who obtain low or 'fail' marks in their written work;

3. those who fail to contribute to tutorial groups;
4. those who do not or cannot attend lectures and tutorials;
5. those who have received official warnings that they are at risk of being required to withdraw from the institution on academic grounds;
6. those who are suffering from examination anxiety;
7. those who have come to a juddering halt at a crucial time in revision for important examinations;
8. those who are disillusioned with the subjects they have chosen;
9. those who find it difficult to choose which subjects to study in the first place, either because none appeal to them or because so many do;
10. those who are in the process of deciding whether to change their subjects;
11. those who chronically or acutely experience feelings of academic inadequacy and believe that they quite simply lack the necessary intellectual equipment for study at this level;
12. those who (often students of 'mature' age) despite their conscientiousness, seem unable to meet academic requirements in either the form or the content of their written work;
13. those who feel strangely unable to maintain motivation enough (even though they may feel committed to achieving the highest standard of knowledge in a chosen subject) to concentrate for more than a minimal time on the essential tasks of reading and writing;
14. those who suspect some physical basis for a general inability to concentrate on or to retain even the simplest bits of knowledge or concepts;
15. those who find themselves displaying physical symptoms in response to academic pressure, whether it be an uncontrollable tremor when attempting to write, or feelings of nausea when in a lecture room, or a fear reaction when in a discussion group, or actual fainting when in any teaching situation.

Commonly several of these will be clustered together within a single referral. Any one of them, if its impact is sufficiently potent, may gradually or impulsively lead a student to get out of university altogether, and to decide quite happily, and with much insight, to forgo the chance of achieving degree or diploma status and to leave for a different sort and level of education at another institution. Or he may decide to leave to enter the practical employment that has increasingly attracted him. Or, and not least important, he may leave for deliberate unemployment because he feels that it would be hypocritical and a sheer waste of everybody's time and energy, not least his own, to remain at university. Those that come to similar decisions, but less happily, find the accompanying stigma 'drop-out', and their own realisation, valid or not, of inadequacy and failure an embittering experience and, at the extreme, it comprises yet another step in a dreadful argument for suicide. Generally, though, the majority presenting such concerns resolve them adequately enough to remain within the university to complete their courses.

CONCENTRATION

Perhaps the most frequently presented 'cluster' embraces difficulties of concentration, characterised by the sort of 'displacement' behaviour which insists that one has worked hard enough today, and that, anyway, there is no urgency for reading that book or completing this essay, that one does deserve a cup of coffee which will only take a quarter of an hour to make and drink, and, of course, it is important that one visits Jane, that there really is a lot of truth in the saying 'all work and no play ...' so leave work for a while and one will come back to it so refreshed that one will really fly through it. The seduction of this not totally irrational inner voice is insidious. It obviously does not matter whether the break for coffee extends to a visit to a friend which leads to the rest of the day being lost as far as work is concerned. But if the next and several subsequent days are spent in this manner the reassurance of the inner voice saying that there is always tomorrow sounds increasingly implausible to the point where the deadline for submitting a piece of work has passed, where nothing like justice can be done to the reading of a key text, and where the shame and guilt at having succumbed to a confidence trick begin spiralling. If by that time, too, the routine of non-work has become too pleasant to break ('after all, nothing awful has happened to me so far') the vicious circle snaps shut. On the rare, impulsive, occasions when intention is fulfilled and an attempt is made to dash off the essay and skim through the text, it is realised that not only does the activity seem to be an intrusion on life and therefore resented, but also that it is just not possible to absorb or to express sufficiently well or quickly the required material. Then the victim may well feel that it is useless trying to concentrate, but that if only he could, all would be well again, that what is wrong is malfunctioning concentration. Thus the problem is neatly isolated and presented as a simple symptom.

Alternatively the presentation of the same symptom may reflect a very different set of circumstances of a very different individual. The over-conscientious student who aims at a perfect completeness of his work and knowledge, who assiduously attempts to work his way through the impossibly long book-list, who carefully and regularly collates his lecture notes in order to achieve this completeness, is not uncommon. His focus upon an ailing concentration may be seen to be the inevitable result of failing to realise the need for selectivity in his studies so that he vainly tackles an ever-increasing amount of work in the belief that it will always be matched by his power of retention and recall. When it is not, then his concentration and memory may be considered to be failing.

It is therefore incumbent upon the counsellor, as always, to listen to the statement of the problem in detail, to find out just how time is typically spent. For this purpose it is often useful to have a client complete an hour-by-hour breakdown of activities of the previous week (see appendix one, pp. 180–1). It can be a sobering experience for a client to see precisely how little, or how much time he has in fact devoted to work, and how much or little has been frittered away on trivia. The counsellor's aim in both cases (having established, we will assume, that the client is asking how he can overcome the difficulty, rather than obliquely expressing non-academic dissatisfactions or indeed that he is not presenting a neurological condition) is to clarify the process responsible for the breakdown of activity and to attempt to reinstate more productive work habits. This may typically cast the counsellor in the rôle of a behavioural engineer, who is encouraging the student to adopt a programme manufactured to his needs, and who is offering himself as a supervisor or director to ensure that the programme is appropriate at every stage of its use and that it is being carried out. Assisting the student to set up a scheme is likely to involve the establishing of discrete daily working periods which are increased over time, though always by manageable steps, to a pre-determined optimum. Apart from the obvious, positive benefits, this may help to reduce the amount of guilt-ridden 'free' time spent by the student, and hence the amount of negative self-reinforcement administered throughout each day. Maintaining a written or mental record of the success or otherwise with which the scheme is adhered to is important if it is to remain appropriate, for by this means modifications can be introduced quickly and meaningfully. Special difficulties might arise before or once the programme has been launched, and will be tackled concurrently. Thus the need might be for a working environment away from the noise and interruptions of a hall of residence, or from the library which does not allow smoking, in which case the counsellor might well negotiate with the administration for the use of a suitable room. Or, better still, the counselling service itself will contain a room which can be easily used for this, and for the many other purposes which make it an important and useful facility. On the other hand, a particular, technical, difficulty might arise, which may seem elementary, such as that of reducing a mass of revision material down to realistically assimilable proportions, or that of discriminating between ways of reading different sorts of material, or that of organising essay material. Then time will obviously be spent in clarifying this particular difficulty, and in *training* the student in a method of approach. 'Training' might indeed extend to the setting of specific tasks which are assessed by the counsellor before being incorporated into the general training scheme. Difficulties concerning the comprehension of specialist material might well involve the counsellor in contacting a member of the academic staff for enlightenment or for suggested reading.

The counselling contract in these circumstances clearly entails much manipulative power for the counsellor, the effectiveness of which ultimately depends upon his credibility. Unlike other sorts of encounter the client is called upon to participate actively in a scheme which is going to make demands upon his time outside the normal 'therapeutic hour', and for which he has no guarantee of success. For the counsellor, too, demands of time might well have to be met outside office hours, for the continuous planning of such a scheme is essential. With some students little time need be spent on ensuring that the plan is carried out and modified where necessary. In some cases it may seem as though the student needs only a metaphorical nudge into such a scheme, having reached the point himself where he realises that he must break out of the vicious circle by some radical change of behaviour and assertion of self-discipline, and is using the counsellor to confirm his intentions and to reassure him as to their appropriateness. For others it seems important to have a sort of 'director' to report to once a week, so that they are not left to the mercy of their own, suspect, will-power to persevere. For others again this sort of programme just will not work. They might try conscientiously enough to put it into effect but find that it is impossible to counter the distractions either of more pleasurable alternatives, or of the superstitious habit (the conditioned response, perhaps) of finding themselves compelled to read everything and of being quite unable to discriminate amongst the material.

HELP FAILS

It would be as well to admit here that 'academic problems' may defeat resolution by the most tenacious and well-equipped counsellors as often as other sorts of difficulties. Where this happens it is incumbent upon the counsellor to make this failure explicit and to decide with his client how, if at all, they should progress from there. It may be that counselling is abandoned altogether, or that it takes a different form by focussing upon another facet of that individual, or that another counsellor, or other sort of professional 'helper' is introduced. Whatever is decided, the way in which the change is initiated is going to contain the same core of acceptance of the client and his difficulties:

    Counsellor: So it just doesn't seem to be working, John?

    Client: Well . . . I suppose not. I'm just sorry I've wasted so much of your time. I still think it's a good idea. It *should* work, but it just doesn't. I just can't stick to any sort of plan. I've tried. I get up in the morning and say 'right! I'll do two hours' reading on history before lunch!' so I feel good at that—once I've made the decision I feel all virtuous—but then I read the paper and talk and then it's time for lunch—then of course I really feel cheesed-off. And it's been like that for the whole time since we started.

    Counsellor: So it's not only not helped you at all, but it's added another dimension of worry—you feel guilty about letting me down as well now!

Client: That's right. (Laughs.)

Counsellor: I wonder what we can do then. It seems to me that we've got some alternatives; we can carry on with this sort of time-tabling, we can chuck it all in and say that you're on your own John, sink or swim, or we can try and think of something new . . .

Client: No, there's no other way. It's up to me. I've known that all the time. I've got to get a grip—if not, well, too bad. I've taken up enough of your time already, it's up to me now. But thanks anyway for trying.

Counsellor: You want to leave it then, John? O.K. but you know where I am—and I don't want you to hesitate about coming back to see me—or one of the others—if you think we can help.

A small extract of apparent non-success that could elicit much critical discussion. It illustrates four things. First, the counsellor's willingness to concede defeat over one attempt at help, secondly, his willingness to continue to try to help, thirdly, allowing his client the freedom to contract out of the relationship easily and fourthly, offering a contract for the future.

STUDY PROBLEMS

Other areas in which the counsellor might well engage in what might be called strategic actions involve specific difficulties with the process of study, some of which have already been alluded to above. These may be grouped into a category comprising reading, essay, and revision difficulties. Taking 'reading' first, a typical presentation would be an expression of failure to cope with what seems to be an unending reading list for a particular course, for if all the books are to have justice done to them it would appear to be a lifetime's work, and not only that, even to read one book at all thoroughly seems to take so long, and further-more by the time one book is completed its contents are almost entirely forgotten.

With 'essay-writing' it is often a problem of creativity. How *is* one to knit together other people's words and concepts into a coherent whole? Even if this is achieved it smacks of plagiarism which is not what education should be about. If an attempt has been made to resolve the dilemma it often seems to transpire that the resulting essay becomes a banal enumeration of other people's ideas, or a series of disconnected concrete statements.

Revision for examinations commonly throws up the problem of selectivity of material and of time, both within the context of perhaps considerable self-doubt and apprehension as to actual performance in the examination situation. It is a time for regret at not reading all the books one had intended, or at missing what are now seen as crucial lectures. Too much material has to be coped with and learned in too short a time.

The extent to which any of these are experienced as incapacitating problems is likely to depend upon past experience. Thus a number of bad examination results and essay marks are likely to increase aversion to study, and to make such situations more difficult to approach with the equanimity they demand, and hence are likely to elicit a poor performance in the future, though not any longer for the same unadulterated reason. So again the vicious circle needs to be broken and 'action' here for the counsellor denotes a similar basic approach referred to under 'concentration difficulties'. That is, after a defining phase during which specific areas are isolated for attention, a process of supervised experimenting and training will probably (though not necessarily) be evolved. Baldly put, some degree of reorganisation of the client's study habits will be attempted. This may entail the setting up of a model of the methodology of reading, revision or essay writing and shaping it to the particular needs and inclinations of the individual. If it is ascertained, for example, that he does read everything so slowly and carefully as to lead inevitably to an ever-increasing backlog of work, then it may well be explained to him how he may learn through a programme of training to achieve a faster reading speed and more productive ways of reading. Whether such a programme will consist of discussion, recommending reading on the topic, actual training and assessment of progress, or elements of each of these, will depend upon the counsellor's judgement in individual situations.

Assistance with essay-writing too, may range from discussion of the efficacy of a certain model, to supervising the reading, note-taking and composition for it. Similarly with revision, help might extend to arranging for the student to sit a mock examination and eliciting detailed comments upon his performance from the appropriate member of the academic staff, in order to get feedback into the system of an objective and modifying sort.

A third 'cluster' emerging from this general heading of study problems for which action seems appropriate contains the less usual 'phobic' type of referral. Action here is likely to be more comprehensive as the training features just described are likely to be involved as well as some intervention into the sphere of the phobic anxiety itself. This is most probably engendered by the examination situation, or by that of tutorials and lectures. A bad performance, for example, in one of the numerous examinations taken during one of his years at university can produce enough stress in a student to induce sufficient fear at the prospect of repeating the failure, and the feelings associated with the process of failing, that all examinations become imbued with a potent aversive quality. The same might occur in the tutorial situation, where adverse criticism and unsympathetic comment can lead quickly to a disinclination to attend future meetings. Where there is no requirement to do so, an avoidance response may be speedily established. Of course, similar behaviour may be rooted in other causes as alluded to in chapter eight, and the individual might well attempt to overcome his fears whatever the cause, sometimes presumably successfully, sometimes with results which exacerbate the original reactions. Some within the latter category manifest embarrassing physical symptoms of fainting, vomiting or of running out of the lecture or examination room.

The counselling procedure adopted in these more extreme cases is likely again to be behaviouristically orientated and perhaps involve both an *in vivo* and an imaginal desensitisation programme. Tutors and peers might in such cases be alerted that such treatment is in progress and their cooperation sought to allow for its unimpeded progress. For instance, it may be deemed appropriate to have a client spend increasing time in a particular tutorial, beginning with a five-minute span, in which case the tutor involved must clearly be consulted beforehand, if only out of courtesy.

Inevitably there is likely to be a 'miscellaneous' group for whom a similar approach seems appropriate; a group though which fits uneasily in to the slot of 'study problems', and whose members present individual, isolated, difficulties to a counselling service. No single method of treatment may seem completely relevant, and yet all may seem to have something to offer. It is worth raising such a case as it will serve to underline further the impossibility of categorising all clients into neat treatment boxes, and the need for counselling flexibility. The case of Les will illustrate the point.

Les, a conscientious, second-year student, enjoyed his subjects, and usually obtained good marks in written work and in examinations. He referred himself to the Counselling Service and presented a problem which he had failed to overcome on his own, and which was making it increasingly difficult for him to get through sufficient work. This in itself had become a secondary source of worry, so that there were now times when even the contemplation of a day's reading and writing evoked considerable anxiety. The problem concerned the pace at which he worked. At worst, and these times seemed to occur at random, he would begin to read (or write) and within ten minutes or so he would become aware that his speed of reading had significantly increased and the momentum that he was gathering seemed impossible to control. Accompanying this was an increase in physical activity in the form of fidgeting of legs and hands. The pitch was reached in less than an hour when the activity became unbearable and he felt exhausted. He would rest for a while, but once he began studying again the process would repeat itself. It was not long before he suffered a headache and felt too tired to continue.

There was no lack of sources of explanation for the phenomenon both from his life experiences and from his present confused perception of himself and of his social and academic status. Nevertheless, despite a traditional psychotherapeutic counselling approach, psychiatric consultation and chemotherapy, the symptoms persisted. Time was clearly at a premium if he was to stand a chance of remaining in the academic setting. The armoury of behaviour therapy was deployed and desensitisation (see appendix one) was applied. The symptoms subsided to manageable proportions, and although it is impossible to attribute the change to any one approach, or indeed to any at all, he did seem able to use the technique of physical relaxation with considerable effect in countering the onset of the disturbance.

SUBJECT CHOICE

Calling for a different counselling orientation are those problems which seem to reduce to (*a*) the difficulty of choosing which subjects to study, applicable in those higher education establishments which allow for delayed decisions of this sort, and (*b*) a disillusionment with the subjects chosen for study, and probably a desire to change them. Again the cause of such referrals may be multi-faceted and the extent of the accompanying anxiety may be of any order. Assuming however that an underlying problem of a different kind is not involved, the counselling process for both (*a*) and (*b*) is going initially to be largely clarificatory, and will later involve the provision of technical data on the career implications of the different alternatives, and upon the method of changing subjects either within the same institution or by transferring to another institution, with all the implications entailed in terms of finance and timing.

The presentation of (*a*) as a problem will typically be, either, that it is difficult to confine interest to one or two subjects, or that it is difficult to generate sufficient interest in *any* subject, or that there is conflict between the individual's preferences and that of his parents.

The presentation of (*b*) will usually be at a time when the student has been finally forced to recognise that the subjects he was good at, enjoyed and assumed he would continue to enjoy (if he had even given thought to it) are now of little interest to him. Such a situation might arise, for example, in the case of the person with a science background wanting to read one of the social sciences, or the arts man deciding that medicine is the only worthwhile pursuit. For them, the change will be radical and will perhaps necessitate returning to the educational stage prior to university to obtain the relevant entrance requirements. For others, less sure of their dedication, a compromise may be needed by utilising their degree subjects in such a way as to place themselves on the periphery of the newly-chosen field. Effective help here is obviously dependent upon the provision of occupational information, and of the details of professional training requirements.

Counselling 'action' in these areas is likely to be confined to discovering from the appropriate authorities the feasibility of such changes and assisting with the strategy of effecting any agreed change.

FAILURE

Failure, or its imminence, comprises the last category in this section. It may be that consultation is sought in order to lessen the possibility of its recurrence, when the counsellor might be involved in the sort of training or desensitisation programme described above; or it may be that it was failure in a crucial examination and the student has been required to withdraw from the institution altogether. Such a case places a characteristic constraint upon counselling—that of time. The client is likely to have only a matter of days before actually leaving in which to explore future possibilities with the counsellor. Obviously they can correspond with each other but letters are not the most desirable medium through which to work. The questions to be considered will typically be (*a*) whether it is worthwhile to 'appeal' against the requirement to withdraw; (*b*) whether it would be possible to transfer to another institution to attempt another course of study; or (*c*) what occupation could be taken up either in the short-term or with the view of making it a career. Often all three need discussion, and often the limitation of time leaves such exploration unsatisfactorily incomplete. The mood of the client too in this situation will often be a factor in dictating the counselling approach; he will hardly be receptive to a leisurely analysis of his interests and abilities and a matching of these to 'ideal' jobs. He has failed, and failed in subjects in which he was relatively interested and able. Often the search will be for an expedient and not for something that presumes long-term job satisfaction. For others, to whom the failure comes as no surprise, the consultation might be for further details and reassurance about alternative work they have already contemplated and planned to enter in the event of failure.

The problems: 2

Amongst those academic difficulties which seem to have no valid basis the most common is perhaps the doubt about intellectual ability. The dilemma can take the form of 'I am bright enough to have gained entrance to the university, but I don't seem to have a comprehensive grasp of my subjects, which suggests that I am not sufficiently bright to cope with work at this level.' Its presentation to the counsellor is likely to occur in the student's first year of study, and is typically a product of the school-university transitional syndrome. At school his brightness may have been unquestionable; and ample evidence will have been provided for it by his examination performances, his presence in the senior class, his masters' comments and his peer status. At university there is less reassurance. Everyone seems bright, everyone has excelled in entrance examinations, academic tasks are no longer done effortlessly, and good marks are no longer automatically achieved. The stage is set for Doubt's persuasive monologue.

Equally common is the referral which takes the rather different form of 'I got into university by chance, I just scraped through on the entrance requirements, and now my worst fears are justified. Everyone else seems brighter than me, I've had bad essay marks and now I realise that I am just not good enough.'

The supplement to both such referrals may well be 'and so it would probably be best if I left'.

It is often useful, occasionally almost imperative, to obtain an objective measure of intellectual capacity. As a few months' academic performance is a notoriously bad predictor of ultimate success or failure in examinations in three or four years' time, it is often valuable to turn to so-called high-level intelligence tests for different and meaningful information. To be able to introduce into the counselling process data which relate, with relative precision, an individual's test performance to that of a cross-section of other students in the country, may in itself provide a sufficient reduction of anxiety to allow for a confident return to work. It may, on the other hand, serve to focus attention upon what had been regarded as secondary problems, or even as non-problems, but which in fact constitute the major cause of anxiety, or of ineffectual performance. The counselling emphasis may then shift on to an examination of and training in study skills, or into a clarification of more 'personal' issues. Alternatively tests may tend to confirm the student's own diagnosis so that ensuing discussions will be concerned with developing the sort of behaviour with which to cope most effectively with the academic situation, or other academic or vocational possibilities may be examined.

THE MODEL ACADEMIC

The other major 'cluster' to be described in this section involves the display of perfectionistic traits. Thus the client has manufactured a model of 'the good academic' to which he increasingly compares himself unfavourably. His failure to live up to such self-imposed standards (for which he can only too easily detect fresh evidence of excellence by listening to the legends of brilliance that abound in such a community) may lead him to a counsellor bewailing his failure to sit among the gods. The evidence of his competence—good assessments for written and examination work—may seem to have little significance in the light of his scholarly model. He may express his dissatisfaction in terms suggesting that he 'should' get better marks, that he 'should' devote more time to his studies, that he 'should' be able to retain more knowledge. He is likely to cite examples of others who do seem to achieve higher standards than himself, and thus he can present a watertight case to the counsellor, challenging him to find fault with the evidence, and daring him to object to the logical conclusion that he 'should' do better.

The potential danger with such a student is that his anxious determination to succeed will abruptly cease to have any motivating effect. He will then find himself in the typical and frightening situation of being quite unable to organise the material for an essay, of finding it impossible to recall well-learned data in an examination, or of being unable even to read effectively.

Such students are amongst the most difficult clients with whom a counsellor has to deal, on the relatively rare occasions that they refer themselves. Often the seemingly unsatisfactory contract of 'support' is all that may be appropriate. Hopefully the determination itself will not fail to produce dividends, and then such a student is likely to achieve even the highest academic honours: but if it does, and if it fails at a crucial time, the reverse may be true, and the failure, accompanied by a cataclysmic emotional reaction will have far-reaching implications for him as a person. A continued supportive rôle, sustained by the counsellor himself, has the value, perhaps the only value, of contributing an early warning of an impending breakdown, so that the relevant authorities can readily cater for its actual occurrence. Thus, with such forewarning tutors' encouragement and provision of, perhaps, individual teaching sessions, medical officer's arrangements for admission to a health centre, and administrators' organisation of a special examination venue, may all be put into effect with vital speed and ease, so that, at least, he is spared one facet of anxiety—that of being the sort of incongruous figure that no one seems to know what to do with, and would apparently rather not have anything to do with, should such a breakdown occur.

Typically, ultimate success as an undergraduate does little to ameliorate the outlook of such a client, and he may well continue into post-graduate work plagued with similar doubts.

Such then are the main types of 'academic concerns'. The list has not been exhaustive, for there are many possible combinations of difficulties both from within this category and straddling the 'personal' or 'vocational' areas. Even so, the diversity of problems within this one category has been illustrated, and although little detail has been included upon the counselling procedures applicable to each, the need for their diversity has also, one hopes, become apparent.

In this chapter the counsellor has been cast in the rôle of the directive, behavioural engineer, of the person who is willing to accept joint responsibility for the attempt to work towards a solution for what are, in many, though not all cases, problems of a relatively circumscribed nature. The choice of approach to these difficulties owes much to those who have written extensively in this field; much more than will be apparent from the foregoing sections of the chapter. Thus mention of 'systems' and 'programmes' and 'strategies' will have almost always contained a hidden reference to an existing body of work. For example, literature on study methods might be utilised in one enterprise, sections of a volume on effective reading might be used in another, an attempt to replicate promising work appearing in a journal article might be made in yet another. But because our concern is to provide a broadly descriptive account of our work such acknowledgements have been omitted: because, too, our emphasis is upon the individual treatment of the student it would be an impossibly large task to detail every particular combination of approach that we have put into effect. Thus we are advocating no one programme, no one systematic approach, to all those presenting, say, 'study problems'. There will be a common basis to each process in that a clarification of the difficulty and of the aims will be an initial goal, and a common thread in that similar literature, or parts of it, will be implicitly referred to or actually used in the ensuing 'programme'. There will exist, too, the fundamental and often repeated manifestation of warmth and understanding in each contact, despite, what for some, will appear to be the imposition of a mechanical and therefore inhuman set of procedures. Apart from the presence of these

E

elements there will be no precise repetition of approach from individual to individual. The concept of a 'workshop' approach to dealing with the various aspects of 'academic concerns' has much appeal in that it allows for economic and intrinsically valuable systematisation. It is an alien concept, however, when it contains the implication of processing people in completely identical ways once a diagnosis has been made. Again, it would be envisaged that some elements of such a procedure would be made common to all (and be made more efficiently), but that allowance would still have to be made for individual differences and circumstances; that flexibility of approach would still remain crucial.

The recognition, too, of the rôle of academic members of staff must be emphasised. Allusions to it have already been made but it deserves to be made more explicit. Without their cooperation and assistance much of the work of the counsellor, in this particular problem area especially, would be less effective and in some cases quite impossible. Liaison between counsellor and lecturer over the student who for good reason is failing to submit written work, or to attend tutorials, or even examinations, is imperative at times if that student is not to be treated dismissively by a department. Of course, the counsellor will be by no means always consulted in such situations, or, if he is, he will not invariably mediate in this sort of way, the student being able and happy enough to establish direct contact between himself and the department concerned.

In other situations collaboration can take a different form. It may be that the lecturer takes on a vital co-training rôle in a particular case, when the need for example is for the provision of private tuition for a limited period in order to phase the tutorial-phobic girl back into normal circulation. The lecturer and counsellor, too, may attempt to coordinate the time-table of a specific programme of work to enable the failing student to recoup academically. Of course, many academics find themselves engaged in such activities without any intervention from the counsellor at all. Some of them do indeed see such activities, and the identification of the student in difficulty, as an integral part of their rôle. Many, however, do not.

As well as his importance as a potential co-counsellor, the academic as a personification of academic success has a different but no less important, significance to the counsellor's potential clientèle. At its simplest level some students' motivation for study and academic achievement is directly influenced by their liking or disliking of their tutors (and this of course can be seen at any level of education whether primary, secondary or tertiary). In higher education this positive or negative regard for tutors is often construed in socio-political terms. It is usually less a matter of whether Dr X is a coherent lecturer than that he is a representative of the type of person and a type of society from which the student feels excluded or alienated. No matter how reputable a scholar Dr X may be, if he is seen as being diametrically opposed to all that the student believes in, the credibility gap can widen to such an extent that the student feels that he can not work for him without sacrificing passionately-held principles. Nor does it have to be as dramatic a basis for dislike as this: the unskilled, hesitant lecturer who finds it difficult to relate to his students on any level at all, is likely to induce in some an exasperated rejection of him as a person and of the subject he professes to teach. It must be emphasised that no generalisation is intended. For many students willingness to work and interest in their subjects remains quite unimpaired by the quality and type of their tutors. For others, the sort of irritations described act as stimuli to succeed despite their presence. But for some, the disillusionment and disappointment can be so intense as to play an important part in failure or decisions to leave the institution.

Clearly there is little the academic can do or would want to do to alter his own personality to command the respect and affection of all his students. It is nevertheless important to realise the continuing power of the much-mocked concept of *in loco parentis* in a student's life. Its implications for the power of learning by modelling are often overlooked; for what the tutor symbolises by both his personal and professional presence is likely to be as potent or otherwise as the way he conveys information about his subject. It may be argued that learning in the sense of modelling oneself upon one's elders and betters, ludicrously old-fashioned as it may sound, is still just as important a function of the educational process as it ever was, even though it no longer seems to be publicly recognised as such, either by staff or by students.

The aetiology of 'academic concerns' is clearly varied and complex. Equally clearly an attempt at their alleviation should be very much the responsibility of the educational institutions which inevitably elicit them.

CHAPTER EIGHT

Personal problems

All problems are personal to those who experience them. It so happens that certain difficulties fall conveniently into categories which are easily recognisable. In this chapter, however, we are concerned with some of those many problems which do not lend themselves to such ready classification. The complex internal world which we shall now enter is populated by neurotic mothers, judgemental fathers, possessive lovers, cruel tutors, hostile students, R. D. Laing, Wilhelm Reich, Friedrich Nietzsche and God himself. In other words, we shall be concerned in what follows with the often nightmarish experience of the late adolescent and young adult as he seeks to find himself, discover a sense of value and of values, relate intimately to others and achieve success along a dimension which has meaning for him.

It is in the young person's search for identity that the counsellor faces some of his sternest challenges. Whenever a student confronts him with an eternal question or the seeming hopelessness of despair he is himself threatened. It needs fresh courage each time to enter the world of the person in existential anguish for one can never be sure what might happen there. And sometimes the challenge is too great. The unknown has about it features so unnerving that the counsellor dare not enter for fear of losing his own grasp on reality. He can only hope in such a case to hold on long enough to muster the necessary courage, or trust that a colleague will provide what he himself cannot chance to give.

Problems of transition

For some students the nightmare begins in the very first weeks of their university careers. The transition from school to higher education is often a painful and difficult one: for some time it is almost intolerable. Bill, a tall but scared-looking first-year man, booked an appointment during the second week of the autumn term. The start of the session which took place serves to throw light on the many anxieties which first-year students can experience and which, in some cases, prove utterly annihilating.

Counsellor: Do sit down. How can I be of help?

Bill: I don't think I can go on. I feel so awful all the time. I don't think I'll ever settle down here. I seem to spend all my time sitting in my room . . . (looks near to tears).

Counsellor: (after a pause) You really feel very hopeless, Bill.

Bill: Yes, I can't see how it can ever change. I'm sure I shan't be able to stay here.

Counsellor: And perhaps you ought to leave now before you make yourself even more miserable.

Bill: Yes, I can't bear it any longer. I feel I shall go mad. (Silence.) But it's all so stupid—I feel such a fool.

Counsellor: You feel you ought to be able to cope.

Bill: Well, other people seem to, don't they Why should I be different?

Counsellor: And yet it seems you are.

Bill: Yes, I notice it all the time. The other blokes in the block seem to be getting on all right. Half of them have got girl friends already. They seem to be enjoying the course—one of them has even been invited to supper by one of the lecturers.

Counsellor: They seem to be part of the place already.

Bill: Yes, and I didn't even really want to come here. I got here through the clearing house. I wasn't expecting to get in this year—in fact, I was just applying for a job when I got the offer.

Counsellor: But you decided to come although you weren't expecting it.

Bill: I suppose so—anyway my father wanted me to come and my headmaster said I'd be a fool not to grab the chance, I don't suppose I really thought about it very much—I'd always thought I wanted to go to university.

Counsellor: And now that you're here it doesn't seem to be coming up to expectations.

Bill: I'm not sure what I did expect really. I'm amazed now how little I'd thought about it. I suppose I imagined it would be something like the sixth form only better.

Counsellor: And you enjoyed the sixth form?

Bill: Yes, I suppose I did. I had some very close friends—blokes, I mean, because it was an all-boys school—the masters were very good and helped us a lot and I was interested in my subjects.

Counsellor: And now it's no longer like that at all.

Bill: No, it isn't. I hardly know anyone here—and those I do know I don't like. The bloke in the next room for example is driving me mad—do you know he plays his record-player full volume after midnight? I don't think it ought to be allowed. And you can't get to know the lecturers can you? I mean, most of them are so remote I'm sure they couldn't care less about me. And the course is so bitty. It seems to be one thing after another and I don't know what I ought to be doing. Some people have written their first essay already but I haven't even read a book properly yet.

Counsellor: So, you feel pretty lonely and wonder what on earth you're supposed to be doing anyway. And the other students aren't very attractive.

Bill: Most of them don't seem natural to me. Some of them look so weird, too. Not that I mind that, really, but I wish they could behave in a normal sort of way. They all seem to be acting some sort of part to me. And if only I could do some work but it all seems so boring and I don't have the energy any longer. Oh dear! I never thought I would get into such a mess—I always thought I was a pretty stable kind of person.

Counsellor: And now you feel lost and don't quite know what to cling on to—and you're beginning to wonder whether it's you or the university.

Bill: Well, it ought not to be like this did it? It can't go on I mean, or else I shall go mad. I can't sleep now and hate going into the refectory. I've got my discussion group after this and I dread that. Last week Professor Green asked me a question and I was so worked up I didn't even understand what he was on about. I felt such a fool. Most of the others in the group seem to be Marxist or something and I can't understand what they're on about either. Is it possible to change groups?

Counsellor: Because perhaps if you changed groups you

wouldn't feel such a fool and might even meet someone you liked . . .

Bill: Oh, it's all so hopeless . . .

Bill's plight has countless strands but in one way or another his experience is paralleled by many students every year. Like Michael to whom we referred in the opening chapter (p. 5) he is a victim of the educational conveyor belt. He is intelligent: a successful sixth-form pupil with ambitious parents and supportive teachers. It has never occurred to him to question the value for him of a university education nor to wonder overmuch what such an education might entail. He has made a decision by default and he has arrived in the university simply because someone else dropped out at the last minute and made the opportunity available. It is difficult to imagine a more inadequate preparation for an experience which will cover one of the most crucially impressionable periods of his life. And yet we as a society allow this mindless drift into higher education to continue year by year without apparent thought for the unfortunate individuals who will pay the price for such irresponsibility by their intense depression and bewilderment. What is more, for the student to retreat at this stage is to risk the charge of 'failure' or 'drop-out' and many, rather than face such ignominy, will struggle on without daring to analyse too closely what it is that makes them choose to go on being miserable and often cruelly lonely.

Bill's lack of personal involvement in the process which washed him up at university is reflected in other aspects of his unhappiness. It is clear that he has no convincing sense of his own identity once he is released into an environment where there is nobody to tell him precisely what to do and nobody to provide him with an instant assessment of how he is doing. Left to his own devices he is unable to plan his life realistically and without the support, encouragement and judgements of friendly teachers, he quickly jumps to the conclusion that he is incompetent and intellectually inept.

The self-denigration extends beyond the confines of academic performance. Bill maintains that the other students are odd or pretentious—as indeed many of them undoubtedly are—but essentially he is troubled by his own inability to function effectively in his social relationships. He tells the counsellor that it is impossible to get to know the lecturers and yet he is aware that one of his contemporaries has already been invited to a meal by a member of the staff. His own loneliness is exacerbated by the knowledge that already others are pairing off or forming closely-knit groups of their own. His inability to relate has therefore been rationalised into a general dislike of the whole student body.

Bill's difficulties have already assumed such proportions that he feels threatened at almost every level. He dare not understand the Marxist philosophy or, one suspects, the other incoherent but passionate viewpoints which are continually voiced around him. To do so would be to reveal to him the unexamined nature of his own life to this point, the lack of clearly defined values and his reliance on accepted custom for determining his own behaviour. It is possible that already he has been teased by a hopeful girl in search of a permissive partner and has not known how to respond. Small wonder that in the face of so many sudden and unprepared-for demands Bill feels that the world is collapsing about his ears. He is almost literally being asked to grow up overnight and finds, not surprisingly, that he does not possess the resources for accomplishing so prodigious a feat.

The implications of the 'Bill syndrome' for schools and the families of all young people need spelling out. It is shameful that such suffering takes place when much of it could be avoided by a proper regard for the developmental needs of adolescents by those who bear responsibility for their upbringing. There may have been a time when it was possible to regard schools as walled gardens in which the young were cherished until they were strong and healthy enough to be let loose on the world. Such a concept of education is no longer defensible if it ever were. Schools need to foster the kind of personal autonomy which can come only if the growing adolescent is permitted to develop those skills which enable him to make decisions about his own life. At the same time he needs every encouragement to explore his feelings, to establish relationships in depth with his contemporaries and those older than himself and to face honestly the confusing array of moral and philosophical models with which contemporary society presents him. No school which concentrates on academic examinations to the exclusion of almost everything else can possibly hope to meet these needs. Perhaps few such schools still exist but we are nonetheless a long way from the desirable situation where schools become the place in which adolescents are free to become aware of themselves as persons and can then rely on skilled and sympathetic help as they strive to grow emotionally and morally as well as intellectually. The cry sometimes goes up that if schools spent more time doing 'that sort of thing' then intellectual standards would deteriorate catastrophically. Perhaps so, although there is precious little evidence to suggest that this would be the case. For the moment the only certainty we can point to is the fact that of those who each year drop out of higher education courses only a small minority do so because they prove to be intellectually inadequate.

Sometimes, however, the school does its best to respond sensitively to the needs of its young people only to find that its efforts are resented or even resisted by parents. It is still relatively common to hear of irate parents protesting that their adolescent daughters are being exposed to obscene literature by the English department. Sixth-form discussion groups which attempt to deal honestly with crucial issues of personal behaviour are attacked as 'putting ideas into their heads'. Even priests have been attacked by bigoted 'believers' for failing to present the 'true faith' when they have honestly—and often courageously—attempted to present Christianity as a religion which actually has something to say about man as an emotional and social being. Parents who behave in this way are doing their children an appalling disservice and are also sowing the seeds of a basic insecurity which sometimes only emerges into full consciousness in the context of the new and frightening university environment. Bill turned out to be such a person. He gradually came to accept that in many ways he envied the behaviour and life-style of many of his fellow-students and dearly wanted to share much of it himself. But he held back not out of respect or love for his parents—which usually produces the kind of healthy tension through which personality is moulded—but out of fear that if he deviated from the narrow and unimaginative way of life on which they had always insisted he would lose their acceptance altogether. Life at home for Bill, it seemed, had always been a contract according to which he received approval only on condition that his behaviour conformed to an explicitly defined and constricting pattern. His school had done little to improve the situation but had merely added—in the kindest possible way—an academic mould as limiting and uninspiring as the social and moral models which were stifling him at home.

If it be thought that we are attacking schools and parents

with an aggressiveness unbecoming in counsellors let us hasten to state that we are doing just that. It is sad that at a time when so much lip-service is paid to personal education and pastoral care in schools countless pupils have apparently experienced seven or eight years of secondary education without once having had an opportunity to explore and express their own needs and feelings and without having had available to them either the people or the data which could have helped them make well-informed decisions about their futures. It is equally sad that there are apparently so few parents around who are capable of passing judgements on their children without implying rejection. Many seem to have given up passing judgements at all which is about as unhelpful as the attitude of the contractual parent whose disapproval inevitably involves the injunction not to darken the threshold again. It is our experience that parents who are so frightened of losing their children's affection that they dare not criticise adversely and parents who offer only conditional approval can have an equally disastrous effect on the adolescent who is grappling with the transition into adulthood. Both responses can create a deep-seated insecurity in the young person which is only fully realised as consciousness expands in the new environment.

Mary suffered from parents whose behaviour was damaging to her for other reasons. She began her student career as a conscientious, quiet, well-mannered, rather timid person who seemed bound for a good degree and an uneventful passage through the University. She seemed very controlled, somewhat lacking in feeling and almost unnaturally precise in speech. There were certain unexpected facets to her which seemed somehow out of keeping with the rest of her personality. She enjoyed mountaineering, for example, and certain energetic forms of dancing. For Mary the pain of transition was unusually delayed. Her first year went by without apparent difficulty: she performed well in examinations, seemed to have settled down reasonably satisfactorily and entered her second year without any overt sign of the storm which was shortly to break.

She first came to the attention of a counsellor during the week-end preceding the start of her fifth term and in spectacular circumstances. She arrived on the door-step of a counsellor's home accompanied by her parents and in a state of physical collapse. The parents requested that the counsellor take her into his home for the time being because she was unable to face sleeping in her own room. They feared that she would have to leave the university altogether if immediate action were not taken to alleviate her anxiety.

Throughout the following weeks Mary continued to display symptoms of physical collapse. She fainted regularly, had difficulty with her breathing, and often seemed on the point of complete exhaustion. She was placed under constant medical supervision and referred for psychiatric opinion. Curiously enough, however, despite these distressing symptoms, nothing physically wrong could be discovered and in other respects Mary's confidence seemed to be developing with startling rapidity. She soon had not one boy-friend but three, she became much less conscientious in her work and yet still produced good results, and most important, as she gained confidence in her counsellor, she began to give voice to feelings which had only recently surfaced into consciousness. The anxiety and its concomitant physical effects had begun, it seemed, when she had come under pressure the previous term from an evangelical Christian group who were keen to capture her soul. This situation had evidently forced Mary, for the first time, to take stock of herself and of her existence and to wonder who she really was. For a terrifying moment she had been made to examine her life and to face the reality of becoming an adult woman. Overnight she was plunged into a momentous identity crisis.

At that point, it seemed, the developmental tasks were totally overwhelming. Mary could not cope and the only way out was to seek refuge in the rôle of the invalid. The puzzle was why she should have resorted to this particular strategy.

Mary: I still keep fainting. I'm feeling pretty peculiar now. Could you open a window for me?

Counsellor: We'll go for a walk and then you won't feel faint.

(Both leave the building and walk in the grounds.)

Mary: I like walking and the fresh air. Perhaps that's why I like mountaineering—it makes me feel strong.

Counsellor: And you like to be able to feel well and in command.

Mary: Yes, I do. I hate being cosseted and fussed over.

Counsellor: You sounded very angry as you said that.

Mary: Did I? Yes, I suppose I was. You see, it's what I've always been used to at home. They've always treated me

as if I were an invalid. Mary do this, Mary, don't do that.
Ought you not to wear your scarf? They still think I'm a
babe in arms.

Counsellor: While in fact, you're a full-grown woman.

Mary: I want to be, you mean. I had a dream the other night.
I was out climbing somewhere—with my father. We came
to a very steep cliff face and I started up it. My father told
me not to be so silly. Of course it was too steep and
difficult, I should fall and hurt myself. But I didn't take
any notice. I went on and I think I reached the top.

Counsellor: Which seems to suggest that you're going to win.

It is not often in our work that we find ourselves risking
such comments as this. In Mary's case, however, as counselling
proceeded it became increasingly evident that, for her, feelings
of security were inextricably bound up with illness and helpless-
ness. At home her parents' characteristic response to her was one
of over-protectiveness and over-concern—and the only way to
become the appropriate recipient of such concern was to fulfil
dutifully the rôle of the sick and weak daughter who required
protection. Faced with the prospect of growing up into adulthood she could no longer rely on her parents' support and
approval and in her insecurity she lapsed into the form of
behaviour which she knew would guarantee her maximum
attention not only from her parents but also from everyone else
with whom she came into contact. It is obviously impossible
to ignore or not to feel concern for the girl who faints in public.

Mary's was an extreme—and fascinating—case of a young
person who is protected from growing up by parents who cannot
tolerate the thought of losing a child. Often the young person
is aware of the problem but this does not make the situation any
easier to handle for to behave as an adult means to step out of
line and to risk losing in consequence the approval and affection
which seem to be conditional upon the maintenance of the
childish rôle. For students trapped in this kind of situation it is
particularly unfortunate that the university vacations are so long
and so frequent. The progress towards maturity is often placed
in serious jeopardy if the student has to spend lengthy periods at
home with parents whose influence is powerful and whose instinc-
tive behavioural pattern reinforces at every turn the rôle of the
dependent child. The counsellor will often be faced by the
student's mounting anxiety as the vacation approaches and much

time and effort must be devoted to the careful planning of the vacation so that the student is not exposed for too long to the influences which threaten his growth.

It is unfortunately true that there are many students whose parents inhibit the growth of their children by offering conditional love or by refusing to face the implications of their own possessiveness and protectiveness. There are others, too, who attach so much importance to academic success that their children find it almost impossible to evaluate themselves in anything other than academic terms. Maureen was first brought to the Counselling Service by friends who were concerned that she was on the verge of what they termed 'a nervous breakdown'. It quickly emerged that they felt themselves to be at the end of their tether with her. It seems that she clung to them tenaciously but offered nothing but a long list of her problems, most of which centred around the impossibility of coping with her academic work and the overwhelming load of assignments with which her 'sadistic' tutors apparently burdened her. She was a pale, bedraggled-looking girl who certainly looked as if she carried the world's problems on her shoulders. She spoke very softly—almost to the point of inaudibility—and her whole manner was desperately shy and inhibited. At first she found it difficult to say anything, but slowly the sense of being completely trapped by her work emerged. A careful analysis of what work actually had to be done and of the time available in which to do it (far in excess, as almost always, of the time necessary for the tasks) did something to reduce her anxiety level. It was clear, however, that the underlying issues had to be confronted if Maureen was to avoid the same kind of crisis in the near future. During the second session, by which time some work had been accomplished and Maureen was feeling calmer and less fearful of almost immediate expulsion from the university, it was clear that she wanted to go deeper.

Maureen: Yes, it's a bit better now but I bet it'll happen all over again next term.

Counsellor: You feel a certain inevitability about it all.

Maureen: Yes, I just can't seem to help myself. I know it's silly but it doesn't seem to make any difference.

Counsellor: You let the work build up and then panic and tell yourself you can't do it and get into a hopeless state.

Maureen: Yes, that's it. But it's silly really, because in the end

I usually manage to get good results and I've never failed an exam. But I do hate it a lot of the time—there was a time when I quite enjoyed my work but now I often want to throw my books out of the window.

Counsellor: The work is so important that you make yourself ill over it but really you hate it.

Maureen: Yes, I do. I really do hate it. I sometimes think that there's nothing else I'm any good for but writing essays and now I can't even do that.

Counsellor: You feel you're not much good for anything, Maureen, except perhaps academic slavery.

Maureen: (suddenly bursts into tears) I feel so hopeless and other people find me such a drag, I know. Even my friends can't put up with me any more. But I don't know what to do.

Counsellor: Maureen, tell me just one or two things you would really like to be able to do but know you can't at the moment. It doesn't matter how silly they sound. Can you think of anything?

Maureen: (at once) I'd like to be able to go into the Students' Union Bar and get myself a drink.

Counsellor: And at the moment you'd be too scared to do that?

Maureen: Yes, I would. I couldn't do it and anyway if I could I should feel I ought not to be there. I'd feel guilty that I ought to be writing an essay or something.

Counsellor: You ought not to be spending time doing anything but working. It's been like that for a long time?

Maureen: As long as I can remember. And when I get home my father always asks me how the work's going and I always say it's going well and then he can go off and tell his friends what a clever daughter he's got.

Counsellor: Your father's proud of you because you're at the university and he tells his friends what an intelligent girl you are. Does he ever tell them anything else about you, do you think?

Maureen: (long pause) I don't know. I shouldn't think so. I don't believe he thinks of me as anything else but a brain-box. He paid me for each O-level I got and when I passed my A-levels he forced me to take twenty pounds. I didn't really want it but what else could I do?

Gradually the picture emerged of a girl who had come to believe that her family—and particularly her father—valued her solely for her intellectual capabilities and achievements. Because of this there had been no incentive for her to develop in other ways. On the contrary it became increasingly important to maintain her high level of academic distinction if she were not to forfeit the approval which she had so precariously established in the eyes of those who were important to her. The university, devoted as it was to the pursuit of academic excellence, was scarcely likely to encourage her to develop other behaviours. It needed a crisis of some magnitude to shake her into the realisation that she was in grave danger of growing up permanently stunted.

Inappropriate criteria for self-evaluation produce a Maureen. For others, however, the value confusion extends to life and security in general. Here again, the situation is often aggravated by a home background where a rigid value system prevails and dogmatic edicts are the order of the day. Dorothy came to the Counselling Service shortly after the beginning of her second term. She was in deep distress because she feared she was pregnant. In fact a medical examination proved that she was not and once the crisis was over it might have been expected that she would have no further use for the counsellor whom she had consulted. In fact, however, she was back within the fortnight only this time her problem was her relationship with her discussion group tutor with whom she had just had what appeared from her account to be a very acrimonious encounter. On the face of it there was little to suggest that the two episodes were connected but both had about them an air of unreality. The pregnancy had indeed turned out to be a false alarm and the conflict with the tutor seemed fairly unlikely both from the counsellor's knowledge of the tutor in question and from the polite and well-spoken impression which Dorothy conveyed by her own manner. It gradually emerged in fact, that what had been presented in the first place as a blazing quarrel was little more than a mild disagreement over an academic point—something which the tutor himself had probably scarcely remembered once the discussion group was over. Dorothy, it seemed, found it necessary to create a drama where no drama was and to cast herself in a rôle which was far removed from the part for which by upbringing she seemed endowed.

> *Counsellor:* Perhaps what you have really been trying to say, Dorothy, is that you would like to have had a blazing row with Dr Smith but that the nearest you could get was a minor argument about a writer's style.
>
> *Dorothy:* You mean you don't believe me?
>
> *Counsellor:* I believe that you would like to have had a row with Dr Smith.
>
> *Dorothy:* Yes, and I would like to have been pregnant as I would like to take drugs and I would like to wear filthy jeans and join Women's Lib.
>
> *Counsellor:* But you won't do any of these things?
>
> *Dorothy:* Oh yes, I will if I can get a bit more courage. I'm sick to death of being treated like a little child and preached to every time I go home or get a letter. My parents are Low Church—always going to bible study groups and the rest of it—and don't I get it rammed down my throat. I think my father believes he's God's chosen representative or something—he just knows all the answers all the time. And the trouble is I haven't got the nerve to tell them to stuff it all and to leave me alone.
>
> *Counsellor:* And you feel that it might be right for you to experiment with drugs and sleep around a bit—but you would never have the nerve to do that either.
>
> *Dorothy:* I don't know anything any longer. I don't know what is right or wrong and I don't care. All I know is that I'm not going to be the bloody horrible little goody goody they want me to be.

Dorothy had been made to internalise a value system which she could no longer accept and against which she had rebelled secretly long ago. Now she needed to spew it out but in the process she was thrashing around desperately for new guidelines to behaviour and swinging violently from one experimental rôle to another. Initially all this was going on in her imagination rather than in reality but gradually as she grew bolder she began to act and once she had started there was no holding her. For her all values and conventions were in the melting pot and she was prepared to face the pain of evolving a new code of conduct for herself from scratch. She left the university more than three years later, rejected by her family and married to a coloured student who had dropped out. She was still very confused, but perhaps a little nearer to finding herself than she had been as the polite well-mannered, piously brain-washed student straight from a sheltered home.

The conveyor belt victim, the over-protected child, the family 'genius', the reluctant Christian—all of them at the period of transition were forced by the new environment to face themselves as people. They faced the existential questions which sound so glib and yet, in reality, constitute the very nub of the developmental tasks which confront the student age-group—Who am I? What do other people mean to me and I to them? What do I believe? What must I reject? What does it mean to be a mature adult? Characteristically, too, the period of transition, because it involves the removal of so many external symbols of security, quickly reveals those for whom the symbols have had no inner reality. As one student put it: 'It's like being cast adrift on a limitless ocean without any confidence in your own ability to swim'.

Parents and schools have come out badly in the cases we have so far explored and the balance needs perhaps to be redressed a little. It would be foolish—and untrue—to pretend that unhappy homes and unimaginative schools invariably feature in the background of our most difficult clients. There are many who, with justification, love and respect their parents and some whose schools have treated them with sensitivity. Nevertheless they come to grief in the new situation. It is usually a worthless and unproductive task to seek to attach blame in such cases.

It also happens that young people can harbour astonishing fantasies about their parents. They cast them in stereotyped rôles which bear very little relation to the actual state of affairs and often the counsellor needs to initiate some reality testing. When this is done it is not unusual for a young person to discover that his parents conform very little to the image he has entertained of them. Such a discovery is only possible, however, once communication has been established or, as is often the case, re-established after a gap of some years. The counsellor can be instrumental in motivating a student to express his real feelings at home with the result that the parents are given the opportunity to enter into the kind of relationship with their son or daughter of which they may long since have despaired. When this happens there can be great happiness for all concerned and both student and parents are much enriched.

For the young person the growing-up process inevitably produces pain, involving as it does the quest for a separate identity and the working out of an autonomous response to the world. The wise parents are those who are prepared for the conflicts and see them, not as a sign of aggression or rejection, but as evidence of their children's coming of age. Such parents neither condemn nor condone. They are secure enough in their own sense of identity to retain their integrity and to endure the distress which they experience both with and for their children. In short, they go on loving and refuse to feel too guilty.

Sexual identity

I wish I had a boy-friend—I shall have to get off campus now that we've split up—When she starts talking to another bloke I just feel mad at her—Do you reckon it would help if I joined the Gay Liberation Front?—He wants me to go to bed with him —My father told him never to come to the house again—My dad says that if I don't stop seeing him he'll cut off my allowance —She's terrified of her mother and gets so neurotic—I look so awful and I can't stop eating—How do you know if you're a queer?—I haven't done any work for days because he's always in my room—I can't bear the thought of a semi-detached and two kids—He doesn't believe in marriage—We went to bed together and it was awful—I do it because I like it—Why should I have to put up with naked men in the bathroom?

We are living at a time when sexual mores are changing and the established sexual rôles are under attack from many quarters. This decade has seen the arrival of Women's Lib, the Gay Liberation Front, the new Abortion Act, increasingly sophisticated forms of contraception, attacks on marriage as an institution, nudity on the stage, permissive partners for impotent men. Against such a backcloth it is scarcely surprising that young people are often bewildered and acutely anxious as they attempt to discover the nature of their own sexuality and to work out for themselves what is and what is not acceptable behaviour.

In a university community the potential both for joy and for pain in relationships is enormous. Involvements are intense and break-ups can be even more than normally harrowing because of the necessity of continuing to live in close proximity to the rejected or rejecting partner. For many students, too, the friendships they form at this stage are their first significant venture into the unpredictable world of emotional relationships. It would be foolish to generalise but as we have seen it often happens that the successful A-level candidate has achieved his success in a lonely world where there has been neither the time nor the opportunity for falling in love. He is therefore inexperienced in relationships, apprehensive and very vulnerable. For others, too, this is the time when the freedom and the opportunities seem so enormous that *not* to seek emotional involvement is to risk the accusation, both from others and oneself, of cowardice, or abnormality. 'If you haven't got a girl,' as one student summed it up, 'you begin to wonder what's the matter with you.'

Not to have a girl, or a boy, however, is a minor problem compared to some of the difficulties experienced by those seemingly more fortunate. For men in love one of the commonest sources of anxiety is the inability to appear both manly and gentle; for women there is the difficulty of showing oneself to be both feminine and strong. The age of unisex demands that the conventional stereotypes give way to a new vision of the multi-faceted human being who is both masculine and feminine, rational and emotional, autonomous and dependent. There is much that is good in this new vision for it enables a man to weep and a woman to argue logically but there can be no denying that for those who are struggling to establish their sexual identities it presents difficulties unknown to previous generations. A girl in her first year illustrated the problem well when she said in a freshers' group that she no longer knew how she wanted her boy-friends to behave. There were times when the last thing she required was a man who would open doors for her, take responsibility for decisions and pay for her drinks at the bar and yet on other occasions she could not tolerate the boorishness which seemed often to be the outcome of a militant 'equality' between the sexes. These remarks were immediately capped by a young man in the group who gave an account of his last two amorous encounters:

'Mary was a pretty conventional person, I suppose. She wore skirts most of the time and expected one to help her on with her coat. I remember once that she sulked for a whole evening because I talked about her mother in public. Now Georgie is just about freaking me out. She tells me I ought to get some experience with other girls as well as going out with her and when I offered to pay for her seat at the Cinebowl the other night she just grinned and told me to grow up.'

For persons who are confident and assured in their sexual identity this bewildering variation in behaviour and expectations is challenging and even invigorating but for the hesitant, self-critical nineteen-year-old the lack of consistency contributes yet another alarming factor to an already stressful situation.

Often sexual insecurity has its origin in the home. Kenneth, a withdrawn, inhibited student who longed for a girl-friend but was terrified of taking any initiative soon found himself talking about his father.

'He was never pleased with me no matter what I did. He kept on telling me not to be so feeble—he was always calling me bloody wet—and once when he found me crying with our dog he hit me so hard he nearly knocked me out.'

Such a father by his behaviour and his attitude made it impossible for Kenneth to conceive any form of manliness to which he could hope to aspire. He became more and more conscious that his father despised him as a weakling and an effeminate sentimentalist and gradually he lost all confidence in his ability to become the kind of man who could ever hope to relate to women. There were even times when he found himself resenting his own intellectual ability and wishing instead that he had been born brainless but physically tough. When he was sixteen the situation became so intolerable that Kenneth ran away from home preferring to face an unknown world than to go on living with a man whose model of manliness filled him with feelings of such abject inferiority and humiliation.

Kenneth at least had a model, however disastrous and inappropriate. For many others the problem is not that of the wrong model but the total absence of a model at all. Ian was typical of many young men who suffer not so much from a breakdown in relationship with their fathers as from a distant acquaintanceship which has never developed into anything which could be called a relationship at all.

Counsellor: You don't feel you could discuss your feelings with your father?

Ian: We never discuss anything. Actually I scarcely see anything of him, anyway, so there's not much chance to. He's an accountant and his work takes him away a lot.

Counsellor: And you feel that he's little more than a visitor.

Ian: I don't know who he is. I'm not sure my mother does

any longer, either. She's always moaning about him never being at home.

Counsellor: So you don't know really what he feels about you and your being at university and so on.

Ian: No, we never talk about it. I don't think he begrudges the money. He always pays up his share of the grant. But I don't think he's really interested at all. He certainly never shows that he is.

It is sad that in a case like Ian's where the father has abdicated responsibility there often seems to have been no other model available with whom the growing boy could identify. In the age of the nuclear family uncles, cousins and grandfathers are seldom at hand and yet one might hope that in the schools young people would find men who were prepared to relate to them at a level deeper than that of the academic teacher-pupil relationship. Most often this seems not to have been the case with the result that young men arrive in an institution of higher education without ever having experienced a single relationship of any significance with an older member of their own sex. Small wonder that with such a total lack of identification they find it difficult to establish criteria for their own sexual development.

For girls the behaviour of the father can be equally crucial. Maureen (p. 113) suffered from a parent who apparently regarded her as an academic animal and little else. The importance of the father's judgement seems, however, to play a vital rôle in a young woman's global perception of herself and particularly of herself as a sexual being. If the judgement is hostile or never expressed at all it often seems impossibly difficult for the young woman to enter relationships with confidence or to feel any sense of value in her achievements or objectives. Fiona presented herself early on in her course of social work training. At first her problem seemed to revolve around her suitability or not for the helping professions but it soon emerged that she was also experiencing considerable pain in a stormy relationship with her current boyfriend.

Fiona: When he came to my home in the vac. it was quite evident that Dad couldn't stand the sight of him. He didn't say anything, of course, but I could tell from his attitude.

Counsellor: He disapproved but he didn't say so.

Fiona: Yes and that's typical. There are times when I feel that really he disapproves of me altogether. I'm not even sure that he wanted me to come to university.

Counsellor: And his approval matters to you, Fiona?

Fiona: Of course it does but I don't know what it is he wants me to do.

Counsellor: I know this is painful for you but would you feel ready to explore it a bit further?

Fiona: All right, if you feel it might help (her eyes fill with tears).

Counsellor: Fiona, if suddenly you were given magical powers and could change certain things about your father what would you want to change?

Fiona: Oh, I wouldn't want to change anything. I love him as he is. No, that's not true. I'd like him to let me know sometimes what it is he's thinking or feeling instead of leaving me in the dark or making me feel guilty.

Counsellor: Is it possible that there are things you would love to hear him say but that he never has?

Fiona: (tears streaming down her face) Yes, yes there are. I would like him to tell me that he's proud of me because I'm training to be a social worker and that he's glad I'm at university.

Counsellor: That he believes you're doing something worthwhile. And other things you would like to hear him say . . .

Fiona: (weeping very violently) Oh God! I don't know. Yes, I do but it sounds so silly.

Counsellor: Don't worry. It matters to you.

Fiona: I'd like him to say sometimes that I look pretty and that I'm a nice daughter to have (sobbing for several minutes).

For Fiona this dialogue was very painful but immensely liberating. She came to appreciate the difficulty for her father—who was at the best of times a very reticent man—of expressing love and approval for her now that she was a full-grown woman. Without it ever being made explicit she came to see how she might well be a serious rival to her mother for her father's affection so that he had to guard himself against his own feelings Gradually, too, she became able to read her father's covert signs of approval and to feel that after all he did find her an acceptable daughter. With this recognition came a new assurance in her relationships with men and a renewed enthusiasm about her vocational objectives.

The break-up of a relationship, if it has been in any way a rewarding experience, must always be painful. Sometimes, however, the distress is so extreme that it becomes impossible for one or both of the partners to continue functioning at all. Often relationships on a campus develop with a kind of desperate intensity springing from an insecurity which is alarmingly reinforced if they fail. It would seem, as we have said, that for some students their first intense relationship with a member of the opposite sex is their first real experience of a relationship at all. Consequently it becomes for them not just an important relationship but the centre and purpose of life itself. They are swept overboard by the astonishing joy of intimacy—as indeed, perhaps all lovers should be—but for them the relationship serves, too, to demonstrate the futility, barrenness and lovelessness of the rest of their past experience. When therefore the wonder is past and the relationship reveals its weaknesses there is nothing left to fall back on. Such people seem often to have no close friends, no security at home and no skills or abilities which they can exercise in activities outside their academic pursuits.

There is a double tragedy here. In the first place it is sad that the experience of intimate relationships has been so long delayed that an eighteen- or nineteen-year-old can be vulnerable to such a crippling degree. Secondly there is the fact that many of our young people seem to have lacked all motivation to acquire skills and interests beyond those which the academic curriculum has demanded of them. In time of stress and confusion they have neither people nor activities to which they can cling until the storm is over. For some an intense re-dedication of themselves to academic study provides some kind of temporary answer but for most this is no solution to a situation where they feel more alone than they ever did before the relationship began and where there is no repertoire of skills and activities available to them by means of which they can alleviate their grief and take up the threads of life once more.

While for some the lack of relationships in the past exacerbates their distress, for others the very intensity of previous relationships can produce its own difficulties. Particularly common is the case of the student who has a boy- or girl-friend 'back home'. Such students often arrive at the University vowing eternal

fidelity to their absent partner but in many instances the strain
of the situation soon becomes apparent. Jonathan was a freshman
who had been 'going steady' for eighteen months before arriving
at the University. He came to the Counselling Service towards
the end of his first term and initially presented a study problem.
He was worried because he was falling badly behind with his
work and seemed increasingly incapable of concentration. It was
when the counsellor began to investigate how he actually spent
his time that the real problem emerged. Every week-end, it
seemed, Jonathan left the University and hitched home—a distance
of some eighty miles.

Counsellor: You go home every week-end?

Jonathan: Yes, I have been—except the first one of the term.
    It's my girl-friend, you see. She gets very lonely during
    the week and I feel I must spend some time with her at
    week-ends.

Counsellor: She would become very miserable if she didn't see
    you.

Jonathan: Oh, yes. Actually I think she finds it very difficult
    altogether with me being here.

Counsellor: And it doesn't make it easy for you.

Jonathan: No, you're right there. I've found it very difficult
    to settle down really. I can't help feeling that I'm sort of
    here on a temporary basis. Do you know what I mean?

Counsellor: That something is going to happen which will
    prevent you from staying.

Jonathan: Yes, and every time I see Jenny I find it more
    difficult to come back. And I'm not getting to know
    people here either. The news has sort of got around that
    I'm as good as engaged and I suppose it kind of makes it
    difficult to get to know anyone properly.

Jenny, it turned out, was a student nurse who idolised
Jonathan and feared desperately that she would lose him. Gradually, too, Jonathan came to realise that he was strongly attracted
to other girls whom he met in the university. They seemed
more articulate, more able to share his thoughts and feelings than
Jenny who was divorced from his new world and whose existence
seemed to prevent him from enjoying his new environment to
the full. And yet the guilt feelings he experienced were intense.
His attempts to 'cool' the relationship proved unsuccessful and
as Jenny's unhappiness and possessiveness increased so did his

desperation at being trapped in a situation where whatever he did seemed to cause pain. When he eventually ended the relationship he had to bear Jenny's hysterical arrival at the University and her histrionic attempt at suicide.

David had a different kind of relationship from the past which made life difficult for him. He had been a pupil at a boys' boarding school which, for the most part, he had detested. He was a quiet person, not at all comfortable in groups and with little aptitude for games. At school he was academically competent but not outstanding. In his last year in the sixth form, however, life had been suddenly and marvellously transformed for him by the arrival of a boy two years younger than himself who had immediately established a relationship with him which quickly developed into a passionate friendship. When the time came for David to leave the school they were inseparable and the relationship continued by means of almost daily letters and frequent meetings in London.

The crisis which brought David to a counsellor was the arrival of a disturbing and dramatic letter from his mother. It appeared that she had 'by chance' found a letter from his friend at home and become immediately convinced that her son was involved in a homosexual entanglement of the worst possible kind. Her letter to David was hysterical, abusively judgemental and demanded immediate explanations for his conduct. The impact on David was devastating. He was at one and the same time angry and frightened, guilty and defiant, humiliated and truculent. Overriding everything else, however, was the overwhelming anxiety that perhaps he indeed, was a homosexual and would never be able to experience 'normal' relationships. His depression quickly intensified and he was full of suicidal thoughts.

Fears of homosexuality for both sexes are common in the student age-group and the counsellor needs to exercise great sensitivity in his response to them. In many cases the fear is the result of retarded emotional growth common in a population preoccupied with academic accomplishments whose members have often been reared in single sex schools. Often the sixth form or even the university is the first context in which the need for intimate relationships has made itself insistently felt and it is not surprising that a partner of the same sex has seemed safer and more accessible to many individuals unskilled in establishing relationships of any kind. With the deepening of the relationship —and the happiness experienced through it—comes the fear that this kind of relationship, and this alone, can bring satisfaction. In such cases the counsellor needs to reassure and to help the student see his relationship with his friend as a sure springboard from which he can gradually begin to test other relationships and develop new ways of responding both to members of his own and the opposite sex.

Sometimes, however, the counsellor will be faced by the 'convinced' homosexual. In such a case if he attempts to reassure, his reassurance will elicit the sort of response it deserves. For the man or woman who feels beyond all reasonable doubt that he or she is homosexual the problem—if there is one at all and presumably the counsellor would not be consulted if there were not—is how best to live in the light of this self-knowledge. It is vital in such cases that the counsellor refrain from presenting his own opinion even if that opinion is of the most liberal and permissive kind. He may perhaps feel that homosexuals have every right to seek sexual satisfaction in any way open to them, that they should 'stand up and be counted' and that they should rid themselves of all inappropriate guilt feelings. His client, on the other hand, may not share these perceptions at all but may feel deeply unaccepting of himself. Or again he may feel capable of self-acceptance while needing to take every precaution to prevent others finding out about his sexual inclinations. The counsellor's task—as it always is—is to help his client explore his own feelings and to become aware of the various courses of action available to him. It is not the counsellor's task to impose his own value judgements even if he feels that by so doing he will hasten the growth of his client.

The withholding of value judgements can be equally crucial as young people seek to come to terms with the many other problems presented by our rapidly changing sexual mores. The models of sexual behaviour available to them are now terrifyingly diverse but the counsellor is unlikely to afford much help if he is known to adopt a dogmatic line which makes it impossible for him to respond openly to the problems his clients are experiencing. Furthermore many of these problems indicate a state of affairs which makes it highly desirable that counselling should continue long enough for the student to come to a more profound understanding of the rôle of sex within relationships.

There is evidence at the present time of an attitude towards sexual intercourse among some student groups which often results in great misery for the individual. Intercourse, according to this point of view, is not something reserved for married couples or even intimate partners. It is a way of communicating with another human being—and it has the great advantages that words are not required and that it is not even necessary for the partners to know each other particularly well. In short, sex is the answer to both the problem of loneliness and that of communication—it is relationship without effort with the guarantee of at least a momentary escape from boredom. In such a climate the quality of one's sexual *performance* becomes crucial. If a young man, for example, subscribes to the view that it makes perfect sense to meet a girl at a party for the first time and to have intercourse with her three hours later in the kitchen, then it becomes a matter of extreme importance that he can get a good erection quickly, penetrate easily and avoid premature ejaculation. For the girl, too, it becomes crucial that she gets the pill that suits her, that she can be quickly aroused and that she experiences orgasm frequently. What is more she can turn to the writings of Wilhelm Reich to convince herself just how inadequate she is if she does not enjoy all these things to the full at least once a week.

Many students who do not wholly share these 'permissive' views are nevertheless much affected by the high value placed on competence in sexual performance. Young men particularly often undergo intense suffering because of what they regard as their sexual inferiority. It is perhaps possible for a woman to conceal her frigidity but the young man who does not make it sexually can fool neither himself nor his partner. There was a time, too, when the man could be reasonably certain that it would be left to him to take the initiative. This is no longer so.

Steve: And then she asked me if I would like to lay her and before I could answer she'd taken her jeans off. There was nothing else I could do and it was terrible. I couldn't even get an erection and she just laughed and told me I'd better get some practice and come back again.

Counsellor: And you felt humiliated.

Steve: Yes. I reckon it will be half-way round the campus by now and I dread meeting her in the refectory. What the hell can I do? It's terrible and I just don't see any way out.

It is unusual for a student to present the problem with such a degree of directness but Steve's intense feelings of inadequacy and humiliation can be paralleled in many other cases. Essentially such students are the victims of a view which in the last analysis sees intercourse not as a sign of commitment but merely as a way of establishing one's competence as an adult male or female.

In such a situation the counsellor's task is a complex one but it is unlikely that it will consist merely of lessons in sexual technique although this may well be appropriate in some cases where extreme anxiety is the result of ignorance or naïvety. It will be surprising in cases where counselling continues over any length of time, however, if counsellor and client do not eventually begin to explore the nature of genuine intimacy and the barrenness of sexual efficiency without commitment. It is undoubtedly true that in many cases where intercourse is seen as the way of making contact rather than as the culmination of a relationship it becomes in the end the very means by which relationship is avoided altogether. The stage can be reached where it is easier to 'make love' than to talk or to share experiences.

Drugs and self-knowledge

The fear of aloneness and futility and the desperate need to make contact drives some to a false reliance on sexual intercourse. Others seek an answer in the use of drugs. It could be argued, indeed, that there is no such thing as a sex or a drugs problem on our campuses at all. There is rather a desperate need for contact and for meaning and it is the search for these which leads some to sex and others to drugs.

It is scarcely surprising that for many the remedy for a need should be drugs. Western civilisation is, in many ways, a drug-orientated culture. Everybody is using drugs to remedy anything from diarrhoea to acute anxiety. It is no cause for astonishment therefore that young people should seek relief in chemicals for the pain which they experience through their inability to communicate with each other and through the sense of purposelessness by which they are afflicted.

The intensity of this pain and the scale on which it is endured is new. Material affluence has brought about a situation where physical needs are met and people are 'released' into full consciousness of their psychological and emotional needs. It is not unusual for students to complain bitterly that on the campus everything is 'laid on'—food is obtainable in the refectories, domestics clean the rooms, sheets are changed and clothes are laundered. The real complaint is that there are not even domestic chores standing between a student and his confrontation with problems of meaning and purpose. 'I hate this place for making me ask questions nobody can answer', was the way one student expressed his anger and his despair.

It would be foolish to pretend that all the 'pot' smokers and the 'acid' takers are seeking to remedy their deep disenchantment with the world and with themselves. Many 'smoke' because it is enjoyable and cheaper than alcohol and a few take 'acid' because they find it exciting and risky. The heavy 'smokers' and the regular 'trippers', however, pursue their activities in the full knowledge that they could be arrested and, more significantly, that they could be doing themselves some, if not grave, psychological and physical harm. Clearly something of tremendous importance is at stake when such large risks are run with apparent unconcern. This something, it often turns out, is nothing less than self-knowledge, the ability to contact others and a glimpse of 'real' reality. The following account of an L.S.D. trip which was given by a girl who could not endure solitude and who cut her wrists when her lover deserted her has many of the typical elements of this frightening quest for self, others and meaning.

Julie: It was wonderful at first because I didn't have to speak. I just knew what others were feeling and that they could understand what I felt. But then some horrible things began to happen. The wallpaper which looked so bright and sort of glowing began to peel off the walls and then the wall itself began to melt and all that was left was a thin layer of cardboard. And I felt that I was melting too. I felt terribly exposed and I knew that this was really me with all the pretence stripped off. I wanted to run away because I felt so frightened and when I spoke I couldn't understand what I was saying. And I couldn't understand the others either. There was no way I could make them understand and although they were shouting I couldn't understand a word they said. Then I went all cold and I knew that somehow I was experiencing death. But the terrible thing was that although I was dead I was still alive and I remember thinking that if this was immortality how would I ever dare to die. I was caught for ever.

Counsellor: And you believe what you experienced was real?
Julie: Oh yes. That was me all right and that's why I know I
    didn't really intend to kill myself yesterday because if I
    had really thought about it I would have been much too
    frightened to face the other side of death.

The 'acid' taker wants the answer to life and death and he
wants the truth about himself. For this and for the possibility of
genuine contact with others he is prepared to risk his health and
his sanity. The 'pot' smoker does not have such high expectations.
He hopes for heightened awareness, a relaxation of inhibitions
and an increased ability to experience his own feelings and to
share the feelings of others. What is so terrifying, however, is the
absolute faith of so many drug-takers that their L.S.D. 'tab' or
their cannabis 'joint' really will give them an experience of
truth. Julie did not doubt initially that her trip was an authentic
experience. Death, she believed, really was like that and external
reality was nothing more than a badly constructed stage-set
mounted on cardboard. She knew now that she was doomed to
eternal non-communication and that the search for self-knowledge
was vain. But yet at another level she did not believe it for she
knew full well that she would soon take acid again in the hope
that she would discover a more acceptable and 'final' truth.

It is important to grasp the nature of the needs for which
drugs are the untrustworthy remedy in order to understand the
fury which is evoked among students when harsh sentences are
passed by magistrates on those caught in possession of or even
pushing drugs on the campus. 'It's all right to knock yourself
stupid with pills because you can't sleep but when you take a
tab because you want to find out whether you're real at all they
put the fuzz on to you. And what if you do sell the stuff to other
people at a small profit? You know that they need it to keep
things together at all and you know that they're depending on
you not to let them down. They don't arrest priests do they
because they take the sacrament to someone who's dying?'

It seldom happens in our experience that a student comes with
a drug problem as such. It is almost certain, however, that those
who present problems of loneliness, unsatisfactory relationships,
lethargy, a lack of purpose, value confusion, an inability to
express feelings and many other crippling inadequacies will have
thought seriously of drugs as a possible answer to their unhappiness. Many will have experimented, some will be regular users

often preserving a blind faith in the efficacy of the drug despite the many let-downs. In a few cases the abuse will be so excessive that nothing can be achieved until the student is freed from the grip not only of the drug but also of the group where his behaviour has been prompted and encouraged. This will often prove almost impossibly difficult because amongst his fellow drug-users the student may well have discovered a kind of companionship and loyalty which for all its deficiencies is far in advance of anything else he has ever experienced by way of affection and belonging. In such cases the counsellor will have at first nothing more than the relationship he can form with his client with which to combat the power of the drug and of the supportive deviant group. It often seems, and is, an unequal fight. Should he succeed, however, in making genuine contact with the student he will by that very act have demonstrated empirically that there are methods of escaping loneliness and futility which do not involve the disordering of the senses in the fond illusion that communication and meaning are the outcome of the psychedelic revolution.

The counsellor's faith and his repertoire of skills

The search for identity takes young men and women into strange and often frightening paths. In this chapter we have explored some of them. The hopes and fears can lead to moments of ecstasy and to periods of utter desolation. The sudden expansion of consciousness which a new environment induces often brings with it a sense of being overwhelmed and a feeling of impotence in the face of the many tasks which have to be accomplished if life is to become tolerable let alone satisfying. For some, obsessed by their feelings of inferiority and failure, the thought of suicide is never far away and for a handful the only method of communication finally left to them is the dramatic gesture of the overdose or the cut wrists.

In such a jungle of emotions the counsellor is in danger of sinking with his clients if he is unable to trust his own subjective experience of the worthwhileness of existence and of the individual life. All the faith in the world, however, and all the skill can sometimes seem to be of no avail and it is the willingness in the last resort to accept his own powerlessness and yet not to feel guilty that enables the counsellor to continue functioning when others retire bruised or exasperated from the fray. It is precisely this ability not to feel guilty which most young people cannot attain in their relationships with each other, especially when the needs of one member are very great. In a university, for example, the phenomenon of the neurotic group is common. At the centre of such a group there is usually a badly disturbed person whose needs are very great. The other members of the group are initially attracted both by the needs and by their genuine desire to respond to them. The more they respond, however, the greater become the demands made upon them. In the end their resources are exhausted and then the guilt begins—they feel hostile and are ashamed of their aggression, they feel impotent and tell themselves they ought to be able to do more. The strain begins to take its toll as they find themselves gradually doubting their own validity, their own ability to relate effectively and the worthwhileness of their own activities. It is not unknown for the supportive friends to collapse completely while the focus of their concern continues his neurotic dance apparently unaffected either by their concern or by their disintegration. Sometimes events can take an even more sinister turn. The feelings of guilt and aggressive impotence are so insupportable that they need to be released. Members of the group will begin to attack each other or, more commonly, they will seek a common enemy who will be held responsible for their impotence and who can take over their guilt and receive their aggression. All too often this means that once a disturbed person has damaged those who attempt to respond to his need the whole group turns in violent resentment either upon the individual himself whose needs they have failed to meet or upon the institution which has somehow allowed this to happen. Tutors, wardens and administrators are seen as the heartless bureaucrats who, because they care about academic work, domestic order and the life of the community as a whole, vitiate by their insensitive interventions the work of healing which otherwise the group could have accomplished.

No counsellor, however, will be able to acquire the faith which accepts powerlessness and goes beyond it unless he is constantly attempting to add to his own repertoire of skills. The complacent counsellor is the one who has ceased to take the needs of his clients seriously, whose complacency is the result not of faith but of a fundamental refusal to commit himself to the task.

Such a refusal is lurking behind the bitter arguments which have sometimes developed between the various counselling 'schools'. The analytical counsellors have scorned the behaviourists for tinkering around with symptoms while the behaviourists have scorned the analysts for inducing insights which leave behaviour unchanged. The group counsellors have denigrated the dyad as reinforcing dependency and inferiority while the conventional counsellors never tire of stressing the dangers of group work and the irresponsibility of the group counsellors. The client-centred counsellors are appalled at the didactic methods of the learning theorists while the learning theorists ridicule the ineffectiveness of the persistent reflection of feeling. The permutations are endless and it sometimes seems that the battles, however futile and destructive, will rage for ever.

No educator, however, can afford to shelter behind his own training and prejudices and justify this in the name of truth or science or purity of practice or anything else. The immensity of the educational task demands a catholicity of approach which can only be offered by those who are committed and humble enough to acknowledge the value of many different skills. The young person's search for identity assumes so many forms, as we have seen in this brief review of the more common difficulties, that the counsellor who has only one approach to offer must inevitably fail with many of his clients. For some students a listening ear may be enough: for others the accurate reflection of feeling will release the tension that is preventing development. Others, however, need to learn new behaviour or to acquire new skills while some must build a whole new value system on which to base their future lives. Most frequently of all, perhaps, there is the need to relate to others in ways which are more contact-producing and more self-enhancing. Small wonder, then, that as time goes by, we come to value many approaches and now embrace a militant eclecticism. If this were not the case the feeling of impotence when it comes could well engender not the calm of faith but the guilt born of sloth or cowardice or just sheer incompetence.

F

PART THREE

CHAPTER NINE

Counselling in a changing context

Already many institutions of higher education have considered the case for appointing counsellors, sometimes in response to the request of students, sometimes in recognition of the fact that the needs of students cannot be adequately dealt with by existing staff.

In chapter three we pointed out that some staff at present in welfare positions belong to an era long since past, when students accepted their paternalistic rôles as tutors of men students, tutors of women students, principals and wardens of residence halls, advisers to students and similar functions. Many graduates owe much to the care and commitment of such people, to their willingness to dispense wisdom and commonsense in situations of crisis which arose then as they do now in the everyday life of students. They achieved a great deal but they and their methods are no longer as acceptable as they were to the present generation of students. In all walks of life professionalism is on the increase. University teaching itself is subject to the same movement with a number of universities having instituted short courses on teaching and lecturing techniques for the benefit of new members of the academic staff.

As older academics in welfare jobs have reached retiring age and new problems have affected the institutions of higher education a rash of committees has appeared to look into student needs and the possible establishment of student counselling services. Unfortunately few such committee members have any real concept of what to expect of a professional counselling service and there is considerable danger of their establishing services which hold little prospect of developing as fully integrated parts of the higher educational institutions of the future. Staff and students are well aware of the need to make some sort of provision for the minority who are seen as difficult, delinquent, drop-outs, drug-takers or the potentially unemployable. In short many counselling services are established to soothe the conscience of the institutions' administrators in a way which they hope will be acceptable to those sections of their communities they are set up to help. In the hurry to plug the gap single appointments are made of counsellors who are destined to be overworked and overburdened by the extreme problems with which no one else feels competent to cope. Unless the temptation is resisted it will be difficult, if not impossible, for these counselling services to be seen by students as more than 'any port in a storm'. If the counsellor becomes identified in the institution as the person to whom the extreme problem cases go, those who fear they are problems but do not wish to be identified as such are unlikely to seek help until the problem has reached an intolerable stage of gravity. Still less is the service likely to be used by the normal, puzzled student in need of a little information or assistance in solving a problem of a less serious kind. The counselling service will consequently fail to exercise its primary function as an educational and preventive force in the institution.

In establishing counselling services universities and colleges must examine their own needs and their plans for growth and development before they can produce a blueprint which will be appropriate for their particular situation. However great the pressure may be to appoint a counsellor to deal with urgent problems it should be resisted until the college or university is able to set up a service which will be acceptable to staff and students, and which will be well enough staffed not only to deal with the most pressing problems but also to accomplish the task of integrating itself into the community and developing a positive educational rôle.

The size and shape of higher education 1972–77

In 1972 the number of students in British universities was approximately 240,000. By 1976/77 the University Grants Committee proposes a total of 321,500 places for full-time and full-time equivalent students to be split between arts-based and science-based students in the proportion of forty-seven to fifty-three per cent; a slightly changed distribution to the one in 1972 and a thirty per cent increase in the total. The U.G.C. maintains that, from the point of view of future employment of graduates, a problem which now commands a good deal of attention, the expansion of broadly based courses is likely to be of value in both arts- and science-based subject areas. From what we know of the often ill-considered way in which specialist subjects are chosen at present for study in university, and the extent to which students opt to change subjects when given the chance, the advice of the U.G.C. makes sound sense both in encouraging flexibility in the preparation of graduates for the labour market, and in acknowledging the importance of keeping subject options open as long as possible. If the recommendations are implemented to any great extent in universities problems will be posed for those who select students and for students themselves who must make more specialised choices after they have embarked on their courses. However much the help given to sixth formers is improved in assisting them with the choice of university and in preparing for the transition into higher education, the universities will not be able to abdicate their responsibility for assisting students with their subject choices as their own institutions grow in size and complexity. This responsibility could well provide an opportunity for the development of counselling services of a kind which will be seen by students to meet their normal, real and urgent needs to make decisions for themselves, to determine the direction of their academic courses, to hold in balance, from a growing awareness of themselves, present satisfactions with future value. Such services will not be able to function without the close cooperation of the academic staff, and they will fail to meet the needs of students if they limit themselves to giving help with subject choice alone and ignore the other personal and often pressing concerns of a significant proportion of the student body.

It may be wondered why counsellors as well as academics should be involved in assisting students with subject choice. Experience suggests, however, that students who express an initial preference for particular subjects of study often feel self-conscious of having to admit to a waning interest to an academic who is obviously committed to the subject. They actually fear over-persuasion either to remain with the subject or to turn their attention elsewhere. Such fears may be unjustified but the perceptions the student has of the academic will influence whether or not he seeks his help. Even those contemplating post-graduate work often consult counsellors before academics, fearing that their sensitive aspirations may appear grossly pretentious to tutors who demand rigorous standards.

Perhaps the most compelling reason for instituting counselling services when the size of the universities increases is the fear that individuals will be reduced to a hole in a punched card, or an indentation on a strip of magnetic tape, as institutions become compelled to resort to computers in order to rationalise the methods of registration, examination and record-keeping. These methods do little to make an individual feel significant. Loneliness, depression and alienation become more serious hazards as institutions grow in size and the task of providing an appropriate education for the potential leaders in society becomes a more daunting prospect. Problems of communication inevitably increase as institutions develop, and efforts to make people feel significant need to be intensified if the casualties and the loss of human potential which occur from feelings of inadequacy and purposelessness are to be avoided.

A number of medical services in universities have estimated the incidence of emotional disturbance in the student population. The figures vary widely dependent largely on the perceptions and the criteria of the authority being quoted. Anything from five to twenty-five per cent is estimated as the number who suffer sufficient emotional disturbance to interfere with academic work. In a projected university population of 320,000 numbers ranging from 16,000 to 80,000 can be expected to suffer in this way. Too often trends established in the U.S.A. transfer themselves to the U.K. with not altogether beneficial results. Although we cannot foresee the growth in size of individual institutions of higher education to anywhere near the proportions of American state universities, it is to be hoped that the increasing size of British universities will not result in a situation where suicide accounts for a growing proportion of the student group. In the U.S.A., out of a college population of six million students, one thousand lives a year are accounted for by suicide, a figure which is fifty per cent higher for college students than for the population in general. These are dramatic statistics which many might be tempted to dismiss on the assumption that it could not happen here. To a lesser degree it can and does. We must not only attempt to prevent the problem growing but devise means of reducing the kinds of stress and frustration which when sufficiently acute drive young people to these lengths.

Objectives of university education and their implications for counsellors

A student's ability to identify with the objectives of the institution in which he finds himself determines to a considerable extent the degree of satisfaction which he will experience at being there. 'What is a university?', 'What is it like to be at university?', 'What will it do for me if I go to university?'. These are questions which university staff are frequently asked when invited to talk in schools. The questions are simple enough but the answers far more complex than can be conveyed in a brief chat with an individual or the time allowed for a talk to sixth formers. There is no concise answer; indeed there is not even general agreement on what would constitute satisfactory answers to the questions. Most staff would give a different response in reply to all these questions and in the process would convey something of what is the purpose of university education. All too often, however, one suspects that the question is given too little thought. It is taken for granted that everyone knows the answer and that it would be superfluous to spend time in discussing the obvious.

It is vital, however, that counsellors consider the objectives of university education and examine the values of the particular institution in which they work in order to be comfortable with their rôle. Often they will be concerned with understanding the conflicts between the objectives of the particular institution and the needs for self-fulfilment of particular students within it. It is only realistic to recognise that life is often a compromise but to help an individual to evaluate whether such compromise is necessary, possible or even desirable in a particular institution requires the capacity to help an individual explore both his own objectives and values and those of the institution. Unless the institution feels that the objectives of the counsellors are compatible with those of the institution they will not be employed; if they are not seen by students as tolerant of those who challenge or reject those objectives they will not be used.

An amalgamation of all the stated purposes of university education would make the task of university educators at best formidable and at worst impossible. Universities, it is claimed, are concerned with transmitting the cultural heritage and the values of the society. This in itself would be no mean feat but the task is even greater when added to it is the obligation to engage in research and in the preparation of the next generation of scholars, to understand the behaviour of man and of nature in ways which can be applied in the world outside the universities and in some cases to transmit professional skills in medicine, law, engineering and the like in a way which will have immediate relevance and yet be flexible enough to meet changing demands.

By some, universities are viewed as necessarily removed from the hurly-burly of everyday life in order to achieve their objectives, much as a closed religious order. For others they are essentially a part of the everyday world, not only keeping pace with it but providing impetus for change within it at an ever increasing rate. Not only must they educate scholars in the age-old tradition, but they must assume responsibility for turning out the kinds of men and women who will be acceptable in the world of industry and commerce, the Civil Service and social services and the many other occupations which until recently have had their own particular expectations of the graduate. Universities usually deny that their primary objective is to give a vocational qualification; employers on the other hand, are often critical unless universities turn out ready-made specialists. Both are basically interested in producing or recruiting men and women of 'character' with a capacity to use their intelligence in creative ways, to take initiative and assume leadership in their chosen occupation, to fit in without conflict with the non-graduate and yet demonstrate that three or four years of the rate-payers' contribution to their higher education has not been wasted. All this is bewildering to the academic specialist concerned with the pursuit of higher knowledge in some abstruse area of pure research, and equally confusing to the bemused student largely unaware of why he is at university and perhaps concerned if he should be there at all, and often unmotivated towards either an academic career or one usually seen as appropriate to the university graduate.

Any conference of employers is bedevilled by similarly confused expectations of the products of our present-day universities. What they expect of graduates often sounds as unrealistic as the combined goals which academics and university administrators expect to achieve in the three or four years at their disposal. University appointments officers are often expected to bear the brunt of responsibility for 'marketing' these ill-prepared individuals in a world which is still only dimly aware of what it can realistically expect of them.

The goals of university education will necessarily be multiple, at once diverse and conflicting, reflecting as they do the varied approaches and ideals of the academics whom they employ. As they grow in size there is the potential for increasing and for reducing the tensions of students searching for a milieu in which they can find satisfaction and fulfilment. The increased educational opportunities and the development of more broadly based courses will accommodate the needs of more individual students with differing aptitudes, interests and personalities; the bigger the establishments, however, the greater will be the problem for individuals, both staff and students, to feel in harmony with some of the goals of the institution or at least to feel they can find for themselves meaning within the confusing and conflicting goals of the institution. Counsellors, no less than teaching staff, administrators and students, face the same prospect of conflict and confusion. Additionally the nature of their work and responsibilities will require counsellors to tolerate the problem others face in accepting some of the conflicts which are unresolvable and helping in the resolution of others which are capable of being tackled constructively.

The diverse goals of higher education and the varying needs of individuals within it make us as counsellors vividly aware of the necessity of providing a diversity of resources not only for students but also for the staff themselves whose fulfilment so much affects the health of the community. Those whose responsibility it is to plan for the next quinquennium and decade require a sense of perspective which allows them to learn from the past while modifying, or abandoning those structures which are no longer relevant to the needs of the 1970s, 1980s and beyond. Their task is to see the community of the universities in relation to society and to plan a total set of educational services which will meet the general and special needs of a university community. Such planning demands more research than it has so far attracted and the involvement of students as well as professional researchers. Although the cooperation of students is difficult to obtain, often because few feel a commitment to engage in this kind of planning, it is essential to find ways of involving them if the planning is to be relevant to their needs and if some of the proposals which emerge are to be accepted.

Because we feel so strongly that counselling is a part of a total set of educational provision we feel it would be inadequate to talk about the future of counselling without making reference, even though briefly, to the future development of other staff rôles within higher education.

Academic and personal tutoring

In the older universities the rôle of the tutor is long established and extends beyond a mere responsibility for supervising a student's academic progress. Even in the older universities, however, the way in which the rôle is discharged varies greatly with the way in which individual academics perceive the function, and with their personalities. Until recently the boast of the older universities that they operate an effective tutoring system which obviates the need to establish counselling services has been difficult to refute. A 'good tutor' is beyond price and there is little doubt that many students in universities have benefited greatly from the wise counsel of such individuals.

Some of our newer universities have developed tutoring systems in an attempt to provide more effective communication between staff and students and to cater for the individual needs, both academic and personal, of their students.

Students rarely find the arrangement satisfactory. Even where considerable care has been taken to determine whether a tutor should be in a related academic discipline to the student, in an entirely different one or whether two such people should be provided, there is still the problem that the criteria for the appointment of university staff rarely include to any marked degree the ability to effect personal relationships with students. Nor are we advocating that different criteria should necessarily be drawn up in all cases, but unless considerable thought is given to the appointment of at least some staff who will be good tutors, the tensions and conflicts for students will grow to an unproductive level.

It is our observation that departments which give considerable care and attention to maintaining an ease of communication between staff and students both through joint staff/student consultative meetings and systematic tutoring arrangements produce a more purposeful atmosphere and greater feelings of fulfilment for their students.

Some staff enjoy and are even jealous of their relationship with students in a personal tutoring rôle. Others resent and would describe as unwarranted intrusion on their time and on the student's privacy any function over and above their research and lecturing commitments. There will always be these conflicts in departments to be partially resolved or at least tolerated by a flexible promotion structure which does not depend solely on the 'publish or perish' premise of so many American institutions of learning. It might also be possible to ensure the appointment of individuals likely to be more effective in a personal tutoring relationship with students if academic appointments are made not singly in a department but, on occasion, in pairs so that complementary qualifications, skills and qualities can be acquired.

If counsellors are appointed in adequate numbers it should be possible in future to design seminars and start courses for those academics who wish to improve their understanding of students and their capacity to assist them in those affective aspects of their development which impinge on academic achievement.

The University Grants Committee have long declared their interest in helping teachers in higher education to improve their teaching procedures. Short courses have been run at some universities in which counsellors have been involved to alert new staff to the broader needs of students. It should ultimately be possible for counselling staff in every institution to share in such courses of preparation and to devise other means of assisting staff to be more effective tutors.

THE ADMINISTRATION

Those officers of an institution of higher education whose function is described as administrative usually include the vice-chancellor, or principal, the registrar and his staff, the senior tutor or registrar of admissions and examinations and the finance officer. With the growth in size of institutions the possibility of students 'knowing' such people becomes increasingly difficult. To them is attributed the power to grant or withhold privileges and opportunities; to instigate or impede reform.

These shadowy figures of authority act as convenient projections for staff and students alike of the parental and authority figures experienced in childhood. Although the nature of university government often deprives them of a forceful reforming rôle they are often at one and the same time castigated for failing to give firm leadership and for assuming a powerful reactionary hold over university development. The Select Committee of the House of Commons investigating staff/student relations did more than perhaps any other single body to reinforce the stereotype of the authority figure and little if anything to dispel the myths.

Whilst the shape of university government and the size of their allocated budgets exercises a large measure of control over their decision-making capacity there is little doubt that administrators greatly affect the tone of an institution, the priorities given to the various activities within it and the support which the rest of the university community enjoys. This is most certainly true for the counselling function in higher education. Competing as it does for a share of the academic budget it stands no chance of getting under way let alone developing as an essential part of the academic enterprise without the understanding, faith and support of the principal administrators. In other words, the principal administrators of any college where counselling services are to be effectively introduced must be committed to a concept of education which embraces the affective as well as the cognitive development of its students.

Just as in their individual counselling relationships counsellors can assist students to a greater understanding of parental behaviour even though they may not approve it, so, too, they may assist in the mutual understanding between administrators and students. Counsellors are in an unique position to assist in dispelling myths, in breaking down stereotypes which get in the way of improving communication and to feed in to administrators the kind of information culled from their insights into students' behaviour and needs which will assist more constructive planning. This will only be possible if their professional skills and behaviour command the respect of administrators.

THE RANGE OF WELFARE SERVICES

A major factor governing the organisation of welfare services is the provision of residential accommodation. Where a large proportion of students remain at home for their education less attention is given to the provision of medical services, residential and other staff concerned with both discipline and welfare and so on. We recognise that Keele is exceptional in the extent of its residential provision which highlights the need for constant re-evaluation and modification in its operation as the values of succeeding generations of students change.

STAFF IN HALLS OF RESIDENCE

In the space of a decade the rôle of warden in a hall of residence has changed at Keele and similar institutions from one in which the 'disciplinary function' was largely accepted by staff and students alike. Increasingly this disciplining function has been eroded and the conflict within the rôle has now become a source of anxiety and confusion for staff and an equal source of confusion and hostility for students.

As the extent of residential provision grows so the kind of accommodation to be provided as well as the administration of it comes under question. There is an urgent need to explore afresh the place of the residential experience in a student's education before much progress can be made in defining the rôle of staff members.

There is little doubt that, with the increasing size of institutions, college administrators as well as those of students' unions are aware of the need to create in both the academic and social setting a greater diversity of facilities for individuals, both staff and students. The traditional hall of residence with rules to which students pledged adherence before coming up to university, staffed by whole- or part-time academics, is no longer seen as appropriate by either group. Most students seek greater autonomy, a greater involvement in the government of their accommodation, whilst at the same time wanting a staff member to turn to readily in times of personal crisis, or simply when the noise from neighbours' record-players defies their tolerance or intervention.

If the conflict between their disciplinary and welfare functions is to be resolved in ways which make it possible for staff to be seen as people to whom students can turn for help, there needs to be a redefinition of the disciplinary structure and a redevelopment of the welfare rôle. Constant re-evaluation of the kind of regulations which make for ease of communal living is essential and a structure for implementing the agreed rules needs to be set up which involves the student community as fully as possible and relieves the staff of the stigma attaching to the benevolent despot. To the extent that staff are perceived as available to help students both individually on their personal needs and communally in the development of better physical and social conditions they

will have an increasing opportunity of assisting in the development of better staff/student relations and in both the total education and mental health of students. For the future, perhaps, we
may see the development of staff in halls of residence who at
the community level will be facilitators for the kinds of projects
which make for more satisfactory living, and at the individual
level will be available informally to assist those students who
need help and who at least initially do not seek it through more
formal channels. Already some staff in residence halls have sought
training to help them to be more effective in this. If universities
and colleges are to see the experience of residential living as a
part of a student's education there are implications for the preparation of staff which we will consider in the chapter on training.

STAFF IN RELATION TO THE NON-RESIDENT STUDENT

However much variety of accommodation is provided by institutions there will always be students who seek something different
and autonomous. With the projected growth in higher education
there will never be sufficient campus accommodation available
for those who seek it. Thus, amongst students who live outside
the university are the ones who live at home, those who feel
themselves more independent than the rest, those who feel a need
to distance themselves at least for part of their day from the
institution and those who either cannot or do not wish to conform to residential regulations. This group of students not only
needs physical facilities for study and social activities but also
the same ready access to help as resident students enjoy. The
provision of the right kind of help is less easy to organise. The
student who repeatedly requests to change accommodation is
sometimes more in need of a listening ear than another address.
The quietly committed student may thrive in a quiet flatlet but
the social isolate who is ill at ease with himself and even more
uncomfortable in the company of others needs sensitive handling
if he is to survive in the university without breakdown. The
lodgings or welfare officer has a complex rôle which, competently
exercised, will contribute greatly to staff/student relations and
also to the improvement of relations between the university and
the wider community outside.

The student living at home will not necessarily face fewer
problems than those in residence or sharing a terrace house, so
that student union officials, academic and welfare staff need to be

even more alert to the needs of the non-resident student than to the rest of the student body.

For the future there are again implications for the preparation of staff who will be concerned with these students in the total network of services in higher education.

MEDICAL AND HEALTH SERVICES

For many years now universities and some colleges have catered for the health of students by providing on a full- or part-time basis general practitioners, nurses, psychiatrists, physiotherapists and dentists working in health centres whose accommodation varies from barely adequate to lavish in its provision. The increasing concern of medical staff with the mental health of students is reflected in the programme of the annual conference of the British Student Health Association who, in 1970, elected a psychiatrist as their President. Even so, amongst the ranks of student health practitioners there are those who are happier in the practice of physical medicine than in the treatment of psychosomatic illness, stress and depression. As in the community at large, there are still practitioners for whom physical or florid psychotic symptoms make greater claim to treatment than the more lingering not so well-defined ailments which are less responsive to physical treatment. There are those practitioners who make it known that they would break confidentiality were they to be made aware of illicit drug taking, whilst they cheerfully prescribe tradeable quantities of psycho-active drugs. Fortunately most universities and colleges attract to their ranks medical staff who are more aware than many that they can instigate positive approaches to mental health in higher education by such means as researching into the effect of examination stress and the factors contributing to drop-out. A few of them pioneered the introduction of counselling and psychotherapeutic services in higher education and have been instrumental in the development of counselling services outside college health centres as well as educating academic staff in the understanding of stress and breakdown in students.

Physical medicine has gone far in the provision of prophylactic methods and nowhere more so than in higher education. Psychological medicine which is intrinsically related still has a long way to go but it is in this direction that our health centres in higher education have most to learn and to give, not only for the student population but also for the wider community. Counselling services working outside health centres have a great deal both to contribute to and to learn from medical staff. For the future there are implications for the preparation of both which we propose to discuss in the next chapter.

CHAPLAINS

Although active church-goers among staff and students are in the minority, the activities of chaplains are by no means limited to them alone. For the church-goers chaplains are the most active in stimulating staff/student relations and in promoting contact between the university and the church-going members of the neighbouring community. The kinds of activities in which they are likely to take initiatives—Freedom From Hunger lunches, social projects in the wider community—have a tendency to involve many others than the religious. From their particular vantage point they are in a useful position to recognise the needs of the wider university community and they do much to contribute to the mental health of students and staff alike. On the more personal level their roving commission which permits them readily to visit student rooms, to eat with students in the refectories and staff on high table, visit off-camp students and staff in their homes and attend union meetings puts them in a unique position to be available to individuals in need whether students or staff and their families. The enlightened development of their rôle is likely to contribute much to the integration of academic communities.

STUDENT SERVICES

At the stage of late adolescence the peer group plays an extremely important part in the establishment of values. Individual students will normally turn at first to their contemporaries for help of any kind. They are in any case most readily available, concerned about one another and prepared to go to great lengths to give help where it is needed. Their care and concern for one another has always been impressive. More recently they have become rather more organised and sophisticated in their concern for those amongst them who are lonely, depressed, over-anxious and even suicidal. The establishment of 'Contact' groups and 'Nightlines' based on 'Samaritan' principles and staffed overnight by volunteer students is a valuable development. There are numbers of students who early in their lives become identified as the kinds of people others can talk to. A few have themselves become 'drop-outs', unable to survive in the academic world when overburdened by the problems of others. The risk of succumbing to the same pressures still threatens those willing students who volunteer to man a 'drop-in' service for their contemporaries but the risks are more readily obvious to others available to protect them. The pool of caring ability is large and often seen as more readily appropriate and usable by the anxious student. They, as well as the professionals, run the risk of damaging others when they intervene to help in a crisis situation, but the danger can be minimised if they are willing to see themselves as part of a total set of services available to the student, and willing to use counsellors or other consultants to monitor their work without breach of the confidentiality which is so vital to their operation. In the next decade it is to be anticipated that students will become increasingly aware of the needs of minority groups and will be seeking new means of meeting them. Counsellors will need to be sensitive to the value of these groups and available in a consultancy rôle when required.

DOMESTIC, CARETAKING STAFF AND PORTERS

The welfare rôle of domestic staff, caretakers in halls of residence, in lecture theatres and examination halls, and porters in colleges and students' unions often goes largely unrecognised and yet they contribute a great deal to the mental health of a campus community. They come to know the lonely, anxious student as well as the flamboyant poseur who may respond to their authority and discipline when that of the vice-chancellor would be flouted. They have a valuable contribution to make to discussion and seminars on community concerns and are likely to provide insights on behaviour which might otherwise go unnoticed.

The counsellor and his relationship to the total institution of the future

If it is difficult to forecast with any degree of accuracy the future for the more traditional rôles of staff and students it is yet more difficult to predict what will or ought to happen to the rôle of newly established counselling services. However we conceptualise the ideal model of a counselling service its actual scope and operation will be determined by the extent to which newly appointed counsellors demonstrate that they can fulfil the expectations of staff and students responsible for their appointment and, at the same time, add a new dimension to higher education which will be sufficiently well recognised and valued to be allowed to develop.

The nature and size of counselling services will obviously be affected by the growth in size and the change in direction which can be expected by the end of the decade. The changing needs of students as they face the modified demands of higher education will again affect the nature of the counselling provision, as will the changing social conditions, mores and values of society. Perhaps the greatest modifying force of all of the traditional rôles of everyone in education by the end of the decade, whether teacher, administrator, student or counsellor, will be the application of more varied uses of the computer. Already it has had considerable impact on procedures of administration, of registration, record-keeping, financial administration and the like. The computer's future application to the process of decision-making both in planning the size and nature of the university and in enabling individual students to make choices of courses and of occupations is largely unexplored. The recent parliamentary decision to allocate £2 million to research into the application of computers in education will pave the way for new developments. There will be many processes at present carried out by all of us which will be better performed by a computer. The implications for staff in universities are at the same time exciting and threatening. Those who have relied heavily on memory to provide information will be outmoded if not redundant and, as one American student remarked 'those counsellors who behave like computers will be replaced by computers'.

So what is to be the special contribution of the counsellor to higher education? We have already outlined the responsibility of the counsellor in the educational, vocational and personal development of students. If computers are to handle the information-giving elements more effectively, then counsellors will be released for those aspects of human communication at the individual, group and community level with which computers cannot deal. They will need to become more competent in the understanding of the developmental needs of students about which there is an ever increasing amount to know, more skilled in the understanding of human development, the effect of the environment on the individual, in the degree to which computers, psychological tests, and other resources can assist the total education of students. In particular they must become skilled in effecting relationships and using techniques which will assist the integration of the cognitive and affective growth of students. Surely this is what many readers expect to be the responsibilities of the good teacher? Ideally this is so and if perfection is attainable this will be the case. But just as we require teachers to help students to use their mother-tongue more effectively, so there is a need for specialists in human behaviour to assist teachers and students in the learning process. Just as the new sociological subjects are at present to the whole academic spectrum, so counselling is to the total educational activity. Our knowledge of human behaviour is growing, our need to apply it creatively in the interests of the education and mental health of our most able young people is unquestionable.

It is obviously impossible to embody in the person of a single counsellor all the qualities and competencies required to assist all young people in questions and concerns relating to their development. It is, however, possible within a team structure to incorporate a range of personnel with a certain basic understanding and specialisation in human development, each with different competencies to contribute to the total counselling exercise, to the individual and group counselling of students, to the coordination of their efforts with other personnel in the institution and to the in-service training of those staff and students in the community who share their concern for continuously improving their effectiveness.

It is hardly necessary to labour the point that the form of education in which counsellors engage is different from the academic exercise of colleagues. It demands intense involvement with people and at the same time requires its practitioners to be familiar with recent developments in the professional field of counselling. This can only be achieved if administrators are not only aware of this but value and support the counsellor's efforts to improve his knowledge and skills through continuing formal and informal study.

CHAPTER TEN

The selection and preparation of student counsellors

Until 1971, when a course for student counsellors began in a small way at the University of Aston, there had been no specially designed course in Great Britain for those preparing to counsel in higher education. A few students who joined the Keele Institute of Education course which prepares counsellors for work in secondary schools have followed a seminar in Issues in Student Counselling and Case Studies and have also undertaken supervised practicum training with the Keele counsellors. A number of these people are now counselling in higher education but the vast majority now practising counselling with college students owe their training to psychiatric social work, to psychoanalysis, to marriage counselling, to educational and clinical psychology or to secondary school counselling. The slant of the service they are able to provide is necessarily affected by their initial orientation and if they are to move to the kind of model we have described there is considerable need for opportunities of ongoing training. If the counselling profession is to become worthy of the name, it will have rapidly to identify its training needs and standards both for those intending to enter this kind of work and for those already in it. At the present moment the training of counsellors is dispersed uneconomically over a large number of centres, none of which is properly equipped to give a complete preparation for counselling in higher education of the kind we would consider even basic for practising as a professional.

We have reached the stage in the United Kingdom when what is needed is an Institute of Human Relations in Education which will be concerned with the provision of basic courses for those who will function as counsellors, as university appointments officers, as directors of residence halls, as college chaplains, school counsellors, careers officers and the like. The present proliferation of courses is not only wasteful but misses a vital opportunity for all those whose work will contribute to human development in education to develop the common understanding and respect for one another's functions which studying and conferring together would promote. There are undoubtedly a number of courses of study which these differing groups could share and which do not require the same individual supervision which the more specialised forms of practical training demand. Courses in developmental psychology, in psychometrics, in research methods, and in mental health are obvious examples. There are other courses which are particular to the special needs of the individual professional groups. Such courses might be in curriculum development, in teaching methods, in occupational analysis and classification, in manpower planning, in the psychology of special groups such as the gifted, the delinquent or the physically handicapped. Such an idea is not new. In the field of mental health the Tavistock Institute of Human Relations has set a precedent by providing common courses of training for doctors, psychiatrists, social workers, industrialists and others. Perhaps nothing short of a government commission to explore the growing need for the professional preparation of counsellors at all levels of education will result in a development of the kind described. What is needed is the injection of substantial funds to found such an institute. Even a fraction of the sum which the Department of Education and Science is prepared to allocate to research into the use of computers in education, £2 million, would enable an institute to be established which could reap untold benefits for both education and mental health in this country. If such a development is to be left until an independent body like the National Association of Mental Health has had time to explore the problem and exert pressure on the government to take some action, there is a serious danger that the still young and vulnerable profession will have been discredited because it has failed to meet the crying needs which exist and are growing so rapidly in our schools and colleges.

Training needs exist for three different groups: those wishing to enter the field of counselling in schools, colleges or the community; those now working in one of these fields who need to revamp and upgrade themselves by part-time on-the-job training or short-term courses, and those who are either preparing or intending to train counsellors for the profession. The courses which exist at present are largely devoid of staff who have themselves counselled, and whilst it is possible for non-teachers to make a contribution to the training of teachers in our colleges of education, it is inconceivable that we should staff our colleges of education entirely with non-teachers. Similarly it seems inappropriate that the preparation of counsellors should be wholly in the hands of psychologists, psychoanalysts, sociologists and others whose basic contribution is made from a related discipline but not from counselling itself.

The idea of an Institute of Human Relations is sadly still in the realms of fantasy and whilst we may be permitted to day-dream about a future we must for the time being restrict ourselves to considering the basic tasks of selecting and preparing the kinds of counsellors who would be fit to enter the model of counselling we have been describing and of providing the ongoing opportunities they need to keep abreast of developments in the profession.

Selection for counselling in higher education

The importance of careful selection procedures both in the appointment of counsellors and in the choosing of appropriate candidates for training cannot be overemphasised. The task merits a careful evaluation of the criteria for effective counselling and more sophisticated methods of selection than usually typify the appointment of academic staff or the selection of students for academic courses. The behaviour of a counsellor once appointed to an institution will be much more open to criticism by members of that community than any other single academic appointment. It must be recognised that he as a person will project for members of that institution an image of counselling which will determine the extent to which he is used, and to some extent his effectiveness.

Our model counsellor must be committed to and excited by the higher education experience in which he must be intellectually competent to share with both staff and students. Unless this intellectual competence is established as a primary criterion he will not be seen as equipped to undertake those aspects of counselling which are closely related to academic achievement, with questions of subject choice, with the improvement of study skills and the treatment of study difficulties. He must not only be willing to accept continuing change in education but must welcome responsibility for assisting the change in directions which from his experience of students and their needs seem likely to increase their fulfilment. He must, in other words, be an educational revolutionary capable of maintaining contact with the more extreme elements of the student population whilst at the same time maintaining the respect and confidence of the academic and administrative staff whose values may be traditional or even reactionary. If he fails in the former he will cease to have a useful rôle: if he fails in the latter he will cease to have a job. He must also be the kind of person who can share discussions with professionals in other fields of employment and can become involved in and appreciative of the satisfactions and demands of their worlds. Not only is this capacity to relate to other occupational worlds essential in a public relations sense to the institution for which he works, but it is also a necessary qualification if he is to begin to introduce students to the infinite variety of opportunities open to them.

To work in the model we have described he must be more interested in the promotion of health than in the diagnosis and treatment of ill-health. There are some counsellors encouraged by clinical or psychoanalytic models of training, or by the elaborate doctoral and post-doctoral programmes of study in the States, who consider it more interesting and professionally respectable to treat the problems of the minority of students who are deeply disturbed than to assist the development of the whole range of students in the academic community. Whilst such an orientation may be valuable in a clinical setting it is totally inappropriate for a model of counselling basically concerned with education.

The counsellor must be physically and emotionally resilient. There can be few occupations more emotionally demanding than counselling, for it constantly requires the counsellor to examine and re-examine his own motives, values and behaviour, to be willing in turn to accept those of his clients, many of which will be the cause of confusion and concern to them, and to retain a proper sense of his own values and his faith in the capacity of his clients, given often minimal and transitory support, to reach satisfactory conclusions.

Without a capacity to establish empathic relationships with others before entering a course of professional preparation the counsellor will be unable to become a practitioner. He would be as useless as a surgeon without hands. Such a capacity demands that he be sincere and undefensive, willing to explore and accept himself, open to being explored by his clients and capable of emerging as a valid and reliable person. He must be flexible and spontaneous if he is to respond in an appropriate way to the many and varied needs of his clients and he must also be able to live comfortably with himself as a changing person and retain contact with much younger people without needing to ape a generation which he himself has outgrown. Before a person is accepted for a course of preparation which aims to give him the understanding, skills and experience necessary to become a counsellor, he should personally have experienced higher education and have demonstrated that he is the kind of person who is capable of living life richly and fully; who, if he has taught, has done more than would normally be demanded of an adequate teacher, or if he has been a psychologist in a clinical setting has contributed more to the job than one might normally expect. In other areas of his life he should have shown himself to be sensitive and unafraid of new experiences. In mentioning the two occupations of teaching and clinical psychology we would not wish to confine the selection of potential counsellors to these two fields. It seems to us to enrich the experience of counselling and the contribution which counsellors can make to the work of a counselling service if they are drawn from different academic disciplines and different occupational backgrounds. What matters essentially is that those who are accepted for preparation are intelligent, competent in communicating with others both intellectually and affectively and equipped with the kinds of qualities we have described.

The selection of these near-paragons of virtue is difficult, time-consuming, expensive and fallible, requiring the employment of different techniques than those usually employed in the selection of academic members of staff or post-graduate students. Firstly the application form for a professional course must be designed to allow the candidate to explain his qualifications and experience and express himself and his values in a way which allows the selectors to make valid judgements about his initial suitability for interview. Considerable weight must also be given to the judgements of referees who will be asked to comment on the extent to which the candidate can be expected to fulfil the criteria for counselling based on his performance to date. Although we as counsellors believe in the capacity of individuals to change and develop given support we are anxious to attract to our ranks those who have the shortest distances to travel in order to achieve success. We also believe that candidates younger than twenty-five or older than forty-five are unlikely to be as acceptable as those within that age range.

Having undertaken the paper pre-selection of candidates we would expose those who are short-listed to a variety of individual interviews and group exercises designed to elicit the extent to which they meet the criteria established as desirable for counsellors. Individual interviews with a variety of selectors looking for different qualities and group exercises of a rôle-playing kind giving candidates an opportunity of showing their ability will perhaps provide the best measures of future success.

THE PLACE AND LENGTH OF PROFESSIONAL COURSES

Since the model of counselling we are advancing is basically an educational one it seems essential that the professional education of counsellors should take place in a university or college where the department of education is committed to a view of education consistent with the philosophy and practice of counselling. In such a setting not only will the values of counselling be fully appreciated and allowed to flourish but two other benefits will accrue. Firstly potential counsellors will be able to share some of their professional preparation with young teachers, with teachers preparing for administrative posts and with others preparing for a variety of specialist work in education. This will allow course organisers to make use of this unique opportunity not only to effect economies in teaching but also to arrange the kind of inter-disciplinary activities which will encourage the development of respect and cooperation among professionals which is so essential on the job. Secondly, the setting will provide a natural laboratory for practice and research immediately relevant to the potential counsellor. Although we are principally concerned here with the preparation of professional counsellors it is becoming evident that other academics and welfare staff who have until now occupied their positions with no other claim to professionalism than an academic qualification and a concern for others will be demanding professional preparation. Education departments of universities have begun to recognise their responsibility for preparing academics to become more effective teachers. It seems appropriate that they should extend their responsibility to include the preparation of other staff who contribute to the education of students.

The minimum length of the primary professional qualification needs to be at least one full academic year at the postgraduate level. This length of time is barely long enough to introduce students to the body of knowledge and to equip them in the skills and the experience which they will need. Much more is desirable but unlikely to be afforded at this stage in the development of counselling in higher education in Britain.

The aims of professional preparation

We are concerned to build on what already exists in our carefully selected students as we seek to produce people with understanding, skills and greater awareness of themselves as instruments of change in their counselling encounters. This can only be achieved by first examining what is implied by such an apparently simple statement of goals.

It is possible to identify five main areas on which the professional education needs to focus:

1. to equip students with a body of knowledge which will enable them to understand the behaviour of their clients, to appreciate what is normal in the behaviour of the developing adolescent and young adult and to be alert to those signs of disturbance which may require specialised psychiatric treatment;

2. to give students a knowledge of counselling theories and the opportunity to exercise counselling skills under professional supervision which will enable them to function confidently as counsellors;

3. to develop further the empathic qualities already possessed by the counselling students; to increase their flexibility, their capacity to accept other people's values; to extend their awareness of other people's lives and their willingness and courage to enter the often alien world of other people's feelings;

4. to give students insight into the life of an institution as a community, an awareness of the pressures operating in that institution and the ways in which individuals and groups interact within it;

5. to give students the capacity to function not only as practising counsellors but also more broadly as educators in the community in which they work.

Whilst the aims may appear simple, the task of achieving them is formidable during a basic one-year course. All one can hope to do is lay the foundation for future professional development.

The methodology of professional education

The body of knowledge contributing to the understanding of young people is slowly but constantly developing. The methods by which this knowledge and the skills involved in counselling can be acquired by counselling students are also changing with the introduction of new film and audio-visual equipment. These changes call for the demonstration of considerable energy on the part of counsellor educators to explore new knowledge and techniques and to keep in touch with the culture of the contemporary student in order to make the experience of counsellor education relevant to the kind of experience which counsellors will have on the job. Above all the counsellor educator must be fully aware of his responsibility not only for helping to convey the knowledge and skills in new and creative ways but for being a good model for his students. His knowledge, skills and professional behaviour will be sufficiently superior to the students in his charge to encourage their maximum growth. He must also be capable of dovetailing the various facets of counsellor education in such a way that students can relate them as they develop professionally throughout the period of formal education. This is the most difficult thing to achieve in the course but it is important, for example, to the counselling student conducting a live session with a young person confused about vocational goals to know from his study of vocational development theory what can be expected of his client at such a stage in his development or, again, it is important for him to know how, when and whether to administer a psychological test to a student concerned about his ability to achieve academically.

A course which aims to develop the counselling student in the five main areas already outlined will contain:

1. A sound appreciation of the psychology of adolescence studied in the perspective of the total life span. This will be incomplete unless it contains a study of vocational development again in the context of a person's total life. As we have demonstrated in chapter six much of a person's sense of identity relates to vocational choice and it is therefore essential to include a study

of occupational psychology as well as of learning theory and of abnormal psychology.

The psychology of the adolescent needs also to be set in the sociology of the family, the peer group and of education. The law as it affects young people and the counsellor's relationship to it in particular as it affects the issue of confidentiality is a relevant subject for inclusion. As students increasingly come into conflict with the law, as we are now witnessing in relation to the use and abuse of drugs, the counsellor needs to be aware of both his and the client's rights in relation to the law. A study of psychometrics and of research methods is also essential, as well as a special study of the intellectually superior young person who will constitute the bulk of the counsellor's case-load. A continuing examination of conflict as this affects the community, the counsellor and his client, is appropriate if the counsellor is to accept his rôle fully. Many American professional courses seem to have stressed a study of the psychology of adjustment leaving the counsellor with the implication that his rôle is more concerned with assisting his clients to adjust to their environment than to recognise, live with and use constructively the conflicts within themselves and the environment.

2. An introduction to a variety of counselling theories accompanied by an opportunity for the student to examine case studies in detail and to try out his skills in the various methods by rôle-playing both with fellow students and young people. There are now a number of films and audio-visual tapes illustrating a variety of methods. These can be used with rating scales which allow students to develop an appreciation of the factors which contribute to effective counselling. Essentially the practical work supervision must be started at the beginning of the course and carried out in very small groups which give students maximum experience and support whilst they risk themselves in trying out new behaviours. The management of the practicum is the most difficult and the most crucial part of the course. Unless students demonstrate that they can be effective in the practical work they must be rated as unsuitable to practise as professional counsellors, however competent they may be in the other parts of the course.

3. An introduction to methods of increasing flexibility, developing empathic qualities, and extending awareness of other people's worlds and values. Group experiences aimed at increasing

sensitivity can make a valuable contribution as do opportunities of spending time in other worlds, in the homes of underprivileged people, in courts of law, in community schools, in living along- side social workers or indeed even in rôle-playing characters who are quite anathema to the counsellor. The use of art, music, drama and film are also effective media for increasing sensitivity and awareness.

4. A study of community mental health and of case studies which illustrate ways in which community resources can be developed to increase the effectiveness of other staff and students in the community. This is essential in order to increase the con- fidence of counsellors to move outside the normal confines of the counselling room and take a fuller part in the life of the community. Rôle-playing and group dynamics have a valuable part to play here, too. Although an extensive study of philosophy and literature cannot be covered in so short a course, it is essential to introduce students of counselling to the important contribu- tions which certain notable philosophers and writers have made to the understanding of man. Many of the young people who will constitute a part of the counsellor's case-load are often excited and confused by the challenging and conflicting argu- ments of Freud and Laing, Teilhard de Chardin, Buber, Sartre, Camus and countless others. In their continuing education coun- sellors will need to keep abreast at least with the language of philosophies and religions currently in vogue. During their professional course an introduction in particular to the existen- tialist philosophers seems to us to be more valuable than an intensive study of Freud or of any other analytical school.

5. An introduction to teaching methods. No matter how good a counsellor is as a practitioner much of his success will inevitably be measured by academics and others by the extent to which he can communicate to them what it is that he is doing and by how well he can teach those aspects of his work and his findings which enable them to be more effective in their teaching. Counsellors must be good communicators and this is no less important in group situations, in meetings, and in lectures than it is in the counselling session.

THE ORGANISATION OF THE GROUP TO MAXIMISE ITS RESOURCES

The membership of any counselling course will be rich in ex- perience of a variety of kinds. Some will have had considerable experience of youth work, others of dealing with emotionally or other handicapped young people in schools and hospitals, or work in industry, social work departments, the youth employment service, probation service or local authorities. Some will be specifically talented in music, art, drama or ceramics, others will have made a special study of religion, philosophy, literature, anthropology or minority groups. Many of the students will have held posts of considerable responsibility. If the maximum benefit is to be derived from the resources which students bring to the course tutors need to be conscious of the unique contribution which each of the students can make both formally and informally to the education of the group.

It is often difficult for students who have previously been expected to be authorities in their own special fields to feel comfortable to contribute in a group where they may feel extremely ignorant and vulnerable. They may also bring with them to the course a need to compete and demonstrate their superiority to others rather than a willingness to collaborate. Competitiveness, defensiveness and frustration contribute to inhibit the growth of a healthy climate on the course unless this can be constructively explored.

The way in which students are assessed and examined also needs careful planning to eliminate unnecessary stress. It is essential to maintain high standards of academic achievement and practice. These can be better achieved if students are encouraged to share their knowledge and insights in class and in private study and collaborate in achieving standards which have been fully explained to them in advance. If examinations are set, results and model answers fed back immediately will not only increase their knowledge but encourage them to help in the development of similar methods in their own institutions.

A great deal of the most valuable experience in the preparation of counsellors is done in small groups which allow students greater opportunity to express themselves in a critical and supporting atmosphere.

THE COUNSELLING STUDENT AS A CLIENT

If the professional education of students is successful it will inevitably lead the student to question his own motives and values, sometimes in ways which will cause him considerable stress. He will be concerned not only with a re-evaluation of his own self-concept but possibly also with his relationships with his family and friends, with the expectations which they have of him and the ways in which newly acquired insights into his own behaviour will have on his future relationship with them. It is sometimes distressing for a student to become aware of the impact which some of his behaviour may have had on his wife, children and friends. Similarly he will become aware that some of his professional behaviour which was perfectly acceptable and expected of him in his previous rôle will need to be changed or modified if he is to become a counsellor. If he is expecting to return to the educational institution in which he previously worked he may need to consider the impact which such modification of behaviour will have on his relationships with both staff and students and the initial conflict he may face on adopting his new counselling rôle. These kinds of concerns are a normal and essential part of a student's growth. The supervised practicum is often the most stressful part of the student's experience but often does not allow him to explore fully the concerns which it produces. The student is often inhibited from doing so by the knowledge that the supervisor has the responsibility for conferring or withholding the licence to practise as a counsellor. Students may justifiably wonder whether, were he to know some of the more intimate of their concerns, he would be influenced in his judgement of their suitability. For this reason it is desirable that each student should have the opportunity of being counselled by a professional counsellor who has no responsibility for assessment in his particular case. Not only is the opportunity of receiving counselling necessary to the mental health of students on the course but it demonstrates the kind of caring provision which counselling educators should expect to make for their students.

THE ONGOING SUPPORT OF THE COUNSELLOR

Many counsellors emerge after minimal and inadequate preparation to fill single-handed new counselling positions in universities and polytechnics where staff have false expectations of what they will be able to achieve. In the first instance those students whose problems have baffled even the most benevolent tutors or whose behaviour has caused the greatest embarrassment to the institution are the ones who have been encouraged or directed to see the counsellor. If the counsellor fails to contain the student and ameliorate the problem he is immediately the object of criticism.

G

If he fails to share with other staff the secrets which have been revealed in the counselling process he is seen as obstructive. If he 'takes on' a student with problems beyond his competency and is unsuccessful he is seen as totally irresponsible. If he does not survive the stresses and strains of such demanding work and have time to develop a more constructive rôle in the college community his service will quickly become identified in the eyes of students and staff as one which only deals with the very disturbed and in consequence will be shunned by those students who most need help.

It is important to stress again the inadvisability of appointing single-handed counsellors. If this is the only way in which a counselling service can begin then at the very least the institution must make sure that the counsellor has a secretary to make appointments for him and to ensure that he is freed from the interruptions of the telephone call or the knock on the door when he is counselling. The counsellor himself must also quickly identify another professional colleague, a psychiatrist, a counsellor in another institution, psychiatric social worker, marriage counsellor or other practitioner with whom he can in confidence share case discussion of clients with whom he is dealing and who raise questions which he needs to talk out.

Counsellor educators do well to recognise that their students are often more vulnerable in the first year of work as a professional than they were on the course. Their concept of counsellor education needs to include provision for regular meetings of counsellors newly on the job to discuss not only case material relating to their individual and group counselling work but also the kinds of institutional problems which they inevitably encounter when setting up a counselling service.

Additionally counsellors need the stimulus of a programme of continuing education to enable them to keep abreast of new techniques and to examine critical issues in counselling with a supporting group.

The education of counsellor educators

No institution has so far taken responsibility for assisting the education of the few people who are at present employed in the education of counsellors. They have been expected to pull themselves up by their own boot strings and often to absorb what counselling is all about with little or no personal experience drawn from practical work; to engage in the promotion of counselling with critical audiences; to write and research on the subject and to prepare pioneer practitioners at the same time. One of the responsibilities of our proposed Institute of Human Relations in Education would be to prepare staff for the professional courses and to provide continuing opportunities to examine the needs of the profession, the development of courses of professional preparation and new approaches to counselling, its teaching and research.

Practical eclecticism

A survey of counselling approaches and techniques currently employed at Keele

---

Client-centred, Rogerian counselling

The Rogerian approach to counselling places great emphasis on the relationship which the counsellor is able to form with his client. This relationship must be warm and permissive and will be likely to occur when the counsellor is congruent (that is, capable of being what he genuinely is in the relationship and not forced to retreat behind a rôle); empathic (that is, able to understand the client's private world and communicate that understanding) and full of positive and unconditional regard for his client (this means that he can accept and welcome the feelings of his client no matter what they are). Carl Rogers himself has written that personal growth and change in clients seems to come because of human qualities in the counsellor and not because of technical knowledge or ideological sophistication. 'Constructive personal growth is associated with the counsellor's realness, with his genuine and unconditional liking for his client, with his sensitive understanding of his client's private world, and with his ability to communicate these qualities in himself to his client.'*

In practice the Rogerian approach encourages the client to explore his feelings and to face his assessment of himself. In this way, thanks to the relationship with the counsellor, he can come to self-acceptance which is the prerequisite for growth. The Rogerian counsellor has an optimistic concept of human nature and believes that every individual has within him the resources for solving his own problems and also a constructive concern for others. The counsellor will therefore discourage undue dependency

* Taken from Adams, J. F. (ed.) (1965) 'The Interpersonal Relationship the Core of Guidance', in *Counselling and Guidance—a summary view*. New York: Macmillan.

and seldom offer advice. His main task will be to help the client explore and clarify his feelings, accept them and then determine how he wishes to grow.

ADVANTAGES

The appropriateness of a basically Rogerian approach to student counselling springs from:

1. the esteem which is conferred on all clients no matter their concern or status;
2. the encouragement given to the expression of *feeling*, bearing in mind that many students will be unpractised and inhibited in this area as a result of an over-emphasis on cognitive processes;
3. the faith placed in the student to determine his own life and make use of his own resources.

Behaviour therapy

The rationale of behaviour therapy is based upon the view that neurotic behaviour is established by a learning process. The argument proceeds that if this is so then neurotic behaviour can be unlearned: that given sufficient knowledge as to how this maladaptive behaviour is being maintained, then counter learning procedures can be instituted to eradicate it.

Behaviour therapy, then, is a method of treatment which aims to eliminate those fears and anxieties which can be found to be elicited by specific situations. In the setting of a higher education establishment its obvious application is to examination anxiety; some study problems; some situational, social fears; as well as to the small proportion of referrals for other phobic-anxieties. There are a number of techniques employed in behaviour therapy, any of which might be appropriate to the work of the counsellor working at any level of education. A selection of three, though not necessarily independent, techniques, may be mentioned here as they would seem from our experience to be especially appropriate:

SYSTEMATIC DESENSITISATION

The basic principle here is that if a person is physically relaxed he cannot at the same time experience anxiety. Translated into practice the client undergoes training in bodily relaxation (aided at times in clinical settings by hypnosis or drugs) which may take six or considerably more sessions. During this time also a detailed analysis of the anxiety-provoking situations is undertaken in order to allow for the construction of 'hierarchies', or lists, of situations comprising the themes of anxiety. A typical hierarchy, on the theme, say, of examination anxiety, would contain about fifteen statements arranged in ascending order of elicited anxiety. Thus the top item might be 'sitting at the desk in the examination hall reading through the first and difficult question'. The aim is for the client to attain this stage via the graduated steps of the other less fearsome items. The items are presented to him verbally, and he is required to imagine the scenes as clearly as possible whilst maintaining a state of relaxation and state of progress through the hierarchy is dependent upon him being able to sustain this state. When this is impossible a return is made to earlier and less-anxiety inducing items before proceeding upwards again.

The technique may utilise *in vivo* hierarchies requiring the client actually to engage in the activity described by items whilst still operating the same rules of procedure.

MODELLING

While using the same concept of carefully graduated steps towards a prescribed goal, 'modelling' differs from 'desensitisation' in that the counsellor-behaviour therapist actually 'models' the relevant item of behaviour which has then to be copied by the client. As an example, the client who is fearful of crossing roads (perhaps to an incapacitating extent) would typically be taken initially to a quiet street and shown by the counsellor how he crosses it. A later stage may be that the counsellor accompanies the client in the task. The top of this hierarchy may be the client crossing a busy city street alone.

ASSERTIVE TRAINING

A technique closely allied to that of 'psychodrama' described later. The focus is upon changing some part of the client's social behaviour, his interaction with a tutor, for example. The components of his usual behaviour in such a situation are examined with the view to modifying them in ways acceptable to the client. The counsellor will then take on the rôle of the tutor whilst the client attempts to interact in the new ways. The new behaviour is 'shaped' during a series of such enactments or 'behaviour rehearsals'.

The selection of these three techniques does not imply that they are the *only* appropriate behavioural approaches. There is no reason, in principle, why aversion therapy for example, should not in some cases be considered as the treatment of choice.

ADVANTAGES

The advantages of behaviour therapy in student counselling are many:

1. it is an effective and economical way of coping with specific difficulties which may be crippling e.g. fear of hostility or ridicule from fellow students or tutors, fear of illness, fear of lecture halls, fear of examinations;
2. it gives a client confidence in the possibility of consciously and systematically changing maladaptive behaviour, and of release from the clutches of external forces and from his own 'temperament';
3. it gives the client certain skills of relaxation which he can apply to himself outside of the counselling setting and which often enhance his confidence in the modification of behaviour;
4. the client can actually witness his own progress through specific changes in behaviour.

Psychodrama

Psychodrama is a form of group therapy where participants enact their problems and concerns rather than talk about them. The central participant at any given time is called the protagonist and those playing the parts of other characters in his world are known as auxiliary egos. Learning takes place through the immediacy of the enacted experience and from the opportunity afforded to the protagonist of experiencing situations from the point of view of other significant figures in his life. The director of a psychodrama group aids the participants in their enactments by employing a number of techniques and skills which have proved adaptable to the one-to-one counselling interview. At present no counsellor at Keele is adequately trained to conduct psychodrama groups but various psychodramatic techniques are employed.

AUXILIARY EGO

The counsellor invites his client to treat him and to speak to him as if he were the client's father, friend, tutor or whatever. The counsellor in his turn responds with the words and behaviour which he believes to be appropriate to the rôle. He invites the client to correct him if he is responding or behaving out of character. In this way the counsellor is enabled to enter the client's world in a direct and powerful fashion and to experience those feelings which may well be experienced by the significant others in the client's life.

RÔLE-REVERSAL

Timing the moment carefully (and timing is the essential skill in psychodrama), the counsellor who is playing the auxiliary ego invites the client to change rôles. In this way the counsellor 'becomes' the client and the client 'becomes' the significant other.

MIRRORING

The counsellor imitates deliberately and relentlessly the client's posture, non-verbal behaviour and mode of speech. He shows the client himself in a direct and inescapable way.

FANTASY MONOLOGUE

The counsellor invites the client to treat him as if he were, for example, his father and then to say to him all those things he would like to say but has never been able or never dared to say. The counsellor does not respond during this monologue. He then may invite the client to reverse rôles and to say all those things he would like to hear his father say but which he has never heard him say.

REHEARSAL

The counsellor helps the client to rehearse behaviour which he wants to carry out in his real-life situation. For example, the counsellor may play the part of the student next door whom the client will invite for a cup of coffee. By rehearsing an episode in this way the client may gain the necessary courage and confidence to attempt the behaviour in the real-life context.

MIME

The counsellor invites his client to communicate his thoughts and feelings not through words but through gestures and movement. This is a particularly valuable technique both for the tongue-tied and for the compulsively loquacious.

ADVANTAGES

The advantage of psychodramatic techniques lies in the power they have to release feeling in a direct and immediate way. They also ensure that the counsellor is forced to identify imaginatively both with the client and with those others whose behaviour and influence are crucial to the client's perception of himself. An additional advantage lies in the opportunity offered to the client for practising behaviour in the secure setting of the counselling 'theatre'.

Group work

COUNSELLING GROUP

A counselling group is a group of people who have problems for which they have requested help. The counsellor will have responded to them initially as individuals in face-to-face interviews. During the individual counselling process it will have become apparent to the counsellor that a group situation might well prove more helpful, or additionally helpful, to his client. This will then be explored with the client and after careful preparation he will move into a counselling group. Counselling groups are not therefore to be seen as an economy of effort nor as a way-in to individual counselling. They are regarded rather as a form of counselling which is particularly appropriate for certain people who have already experienced individual counselling.

The preparation of an individual for a counselling group is of crucial importance. It is essential that he establishes the goals he hopes to achieve through the group and that he agrees to attempt the kind of behaviour which will aid the group process—e.g. he must be prepared to talk freely, to help others in the group to maintain a therapeutic ethos.

Problems which seem to respond well to group counselling are those related to difficulties in social behaviour and the expression of feeling. Problems of value confusion and purposelessness can also be usefully explored in the group setting. The advantages of the group situation seem to be:

1. that as individual attitudes have their anchorage in groups a new group is more likely to exert power for change than an individual counsellor;
2. that the group makes it possible to experience feelings parallel to one's own in others;
3. that the group presents the opportunity for trying out new modes of interpersonal behaviour;
4. that it is possible to learn without verbalising;
5. that members can experience themselves as helpers as well as clients.

The counsellor acts at all times as a model for the group member. He maintains the therapeutic ethos, helps members to achieve their goals, encourages them to be helpers as well as clients. He must be particularly sensitive to resistance and know how to expose it and use it creatively.

A counselling group should meet regularly (at least weekly for at least sixty minutes) and desirably there should not be too much contact between members outside the group sessions. No very shy members or seriously maladjusted members should be admitted until individual counselling has made it possible for them to achieve a level of functioning which will enable them to fulfil their contract as group members.

FRESHERS' GROUP

A freshers' group is set up with the express intention of giving new members in an institution an opportunity to discuss openly with others their thoughts and feelings about their experiences in the new environment.

Such a group can serve as an anchor against initial loneliness and confusion and gives members a chance to establish their own goals and to work out how best to take advantage of their new situation.

Members of a freshers' group respond to an open invitation to join such a group and will undergo an initial interview during which the purpose of the group will be discussed and the nature of their individual objectives in joining it. Such a group will usually meet weekly for about six to ten weeks during a student's first year in the institution.

The counsellor's task is a complex one but includes the following:

(these objectives of a Discussion Group are cogently discussed in a recent book: *The Group Process as a Helping Technique*, Sheila Thompson and J. H. Kahn, Pergamon Press. 1970).

1. to make the group as effective as possible as a means of teaching members about human behaviour—including their own and his own;
2. to enable all members to participate and to contribute from their own experience;
3. to make appropriate links and to point out relevant connections between contributions;
4. to take an active part in releasing discussion at the outset;
5. to be sensitive to the relationship between himself and the group;
6. to combat actively the tendency towards the concealment of personal feeling;
7. to explore thoroughly fantasies about the institution in which the group takes place;
8. to enable members to question previously held standards and beliefs without thereby exposing themselves to intolerable anxiety.

VOCATIONAL EXPLORATION GROUP

The vocational exploration group is an attempt to help those who feel they have little idea what sort of job they want and are anxious about the whole process of career decision-making. Such a group enables members to share their anxieties and to attempt self-exploration in the company of others who are equally anxious and confused.

The counsellor's task is to help members to move towards a more purposeful and optimistic view of career choice and to suggest ways in which self-exploration can take place and appropriate criteria be established. Sometimes the group as a whole will take vocational interest tests and explore the results of these together. Members can also 'try out' imaginatively certain vocational rôles and receive feed-back from others as to their appropriateness. At such a stage the counsellor will often serve as a source of information and will seek to stimulate group members to explore relevant literature and so on for themselves.

The vocational exploration group is usually short lived. It will have served its purpose if group members are encouraged to continue with the process of vocational exploration independently or through individual counselling sessions.

Counsellor collaboration

In a service where more than one counsellor is operating it is clear that much informal collaboration can and should take place. The following strategies, however, are examples of collaboration which are deliberately formalised and built into the practice of the service.

CASE-CONFERENCES

A case-conference can be called at any time by a counsellor who is unhappy about the progress of a particular client. Shared insights often lead to the adoption of new approaches. Such case-conferences are in addition to the regular sessions with a consultant psychiatrist and to those called by the coordinator (see below).

CONCURRENT COUNSELLING

It sometimes seems appropriate for two counsellors to work concurrently, but separately, with the same client. Such might be the case, for example, with a student who is undergoing behaviour therapy but who also wishes to explore vocational opportunities.

COORDINATION

At any given time one counsellor will be designated as coordinator. The task of the coordinator is to monitor all cases where the same counsellor has seen a client four times or more for the same presenting problems. He will read the notes that his colleague has made on the counselling sessions, possibly discuss the case with him and, if he thinks it desirable, call a case-conference. Clearly such a system can only work effectively when counsellors have confidence in and respect for each other. The office of coordinator rotates and the same counsellor does not hold it for more than a period of four months.

EMPLOYMENT INTERVIEW PRACTICE

Some students are abnormally apprehensive about interviews with prospective employers. Their anxiety is such that they dread the encounter and cannot possibly present themselves effectively. In some cases, remarkably enough, such students will never previously have experienced a selection interview of any kind.

Where it seems appropriate students of this type are offered the opportunity of rôle-playing an employment interview with a counsellor whom they have not previously met. This can take place either in the counsellor's office or in a special room where the interview can be video-taped. The student's 'own' counsellor observes the interview and after the session the student discusses his experience with both counsellors. The video-tape can also be viewed.

The opportunity to undergo the assessment interview in this way is often sufficient to enable the student to cope with his anxiety and to see how he can best prepare himself for the 'real' thing.

The same strategy can be employed with students who are repeatedly unsuccessful in their employment interviews. In such cases the rôle-playing session can be seen as a diagnostic technique.

MULTIPLE COUNSELLING

A counsellor may sometimes judge that it would be helpful for his client to meet with two counsellors at the same time. This might occur, for example, when a student feels comfortable with a counsellor, wishes the relationship to continue and yet experiences little sense of progress. The introduction of another counsellor into the situation at this point may produce new insights and energy. Counselling may then proceed for a limited number of sessions with both counsellors present or the client may be happy to revert to his original counsellor or to transfer his allegiance to the second counsellor. Clearly the multiple counselling situation is very costly in terms of counsellor time and cannot persist for a lengthy period. Usually, however, one or two multiple counselling sessions in the course of a normal one-to-one process are sufficient to generate new energy.

SOCIAL SKILLS TRAINING

Exceptionally shy or inhibited students often have great difficulty in conducting themselves in informal small groups. It has sometimes proved helpful in such cases for two or more counsellors to create an informal group setting in which the student can try himself out socially without fear of ridicule or disaster. Such sessions are usually short and intensity is avoided—a coffee break makes an admirable opportunity for training of this kind. After the event the student will discuss what he experienced with his own counsellor. Feed-back is not offered to the client by the other counsellors who take part although they may, of course, discuss their reactions with the counsellor involved.

Miscellaneous strategies

CRISIS STUDY

A student who is experiencing grave difficulty in concentrating or in settling down to work is given the opportunity of working in a room in close proximity to the Counselling Service. The counsellor is then able to visit the student frequently and to maintain contact with him as he struggles to regain control of his studies. This highly practical arrangement which ensures the concerned involvement of a counsellor in the actual work situation is often sufficient to restore the necessary confidence and motivation.

HOMEWORK

The counsellor and client between them set a task which the client undertakes to attempt before the next counselling session. Such tasks will take a variety of forms according to the particular problems of the individual client, e.g. inviting the man next door for a cup of coffee, writing a letter home, speaking in a tutorial, asking a girl out for a meal. The counsellor must take care that such homework is within the capabilities of the client. Successfully completed homework has the power to increase self-confidence and to encourage fresh risk-taking.

IMAGINARY JOURNEYS

Clients who are depressed or lacking in energy are invited to go on an imaginary journey to a place where they would like to be. Two or three such imaginary journeys can be made. The result is often an alleviation of the depression and a greater willingness to explore possibilities for action. Students, especially those in a campus university, tend to become overwhelmed by their environment. They seem unable to extricate themselves, either physically or imaginatively, from the tasks, relationships and geographical limitations which the university places upon them. The 'imaginary journey' strategy can often have the effect of reminding them of life outside the campus and of relationships and places which are more life enhancing than their present situation. It may sound 'gimmicky' but it works.

INTERVIEWING THE COUNSELLOR

The counsellor invites the client to spend a whole session finding out as much as he likes about the counsellor. This strategy is often highly effective in helping the student feel parity of esteem in the relationship. It also gives him insight into what is involved when initiatives are taken in a relationship.

TIME AND STUDY ANALYSIS

Students often experience a sense of being overwhelmed by a mountain of work. The counsellor helps the student to break down this work into its component parts and to determine how much time is required for each assignment. He then assists the student to draw up a master schedule which details all those hours in the day when he is obligatorily occupied with lectures, tutorials, meals, etc. The time left is then available for academic work and recreation. In nearly all instances the time available is far in excess of the time required for all the assignments put together. This simple procedure can have the effect of reducing anxiety dramatically and giving a student the necessary confidence to tackle his work systematically.

TIME-CHARTING

A client who is badly disorganised and who feels that he has lost control of his life is invited to record, hour by hour, the events of each day over a period of, perhaps, a week. From this record it is usually possible for counsellor and client to focus in on many of the difficulties which the client is experiencing. The client is provided with an outline time-chart for this purpose and an example of a completed chart appears on pages 180–81. It is essential that a client is completely honest when completing his chart. Often it happens that the actual discipline of completing the chart each day produces a marked change in behaviour.

This is perhaps one of the simplest strategies available to a counsellor but its power both as a diagnostic tool and as a means of encouraging new behaviours is often remarkable.

TIME CHART*

Name Margaret James   Week beginning 7th January

Fill in the spaces in the Daily Record at the end of each day indicating exactly what you did each hour period.... It is important that you record *what you did, not what you intended to do or should have done....*

Hours	Mon.	Tues.	Wed.	Thur.	Fri.	Sat.	Sun.
A.M. 12–5	12–2 with friends Sleep	12–3 with friends Sleep	12–1 with friends Sleep	12–2 with friends Sleep	12–3 with friends Sleep	Sleep	Reading in bed till 3
5–6	Sleep	Sleep	Sleep	Sleep	Sleep	Sleep	Sleeping badly
6–7	Sleep	Sleep	Sleep	Sleep	Sleep	Sleep	Sleep
7–8	Sleep	Sleep	Sleep	Sleep	Sleep	Sleep	Got up & went for a walk
8–9	Sleep	Sleep	Sleep	Sleep	Sleep	Sleep	Breakfast & read
9–10	Sleep	Sleep	Breakfast & dress	Sleep	Education Lecture	Sleep	Felt depressed
10–11	Sleep	English Lecture	Education Lecture	Soc. Lecture	Coffee in Union	Sleep	Listening to records
11–12	Breakfast and dress	Coffee in Union	Library	Coffee in Union	Education Tutorial	Dressed & breakfast	Tried to read novel
P.M. 12–1	Union	Lunch	Lunch	Lunch	Lunch	Letter writing	Snack & coffee
1–2	With friends	Listening to records	Coffee with friends	Listening to records	Coffee with friends	Felt depressed	Work in room

2–3	Soc. Lecture	Work in room	Library	Writing letters	Work in room	Snack & coffee	Work in room
3–4	Library	Walk round Lakes	Soc. Tutorial	Nap in room	Work in room	Nap	Went to
4–5	Library	Tea with friends	Tea with friends	Library	Tea with friends	Tried to read novel	Sleep
5–6	English Tutorial	Library	Work in room	Library	Walk in woods	Cried and smoked a lot	Tea & read
6–7	Supper	Supper	Supper	Library	Supper	Union Bar	Supper in block
7–8	Work in room	Work in room	Work in room	Library	Drinking in Union	Union	Sneyd Arms
8–9	Work in room	Soc. Society	Film Soc.	Drinking in Union	Choral Soc. Concert	Dance in Union	Sneyd Arms
9–10	Coffee	Soc. Society	Film Soc.	Work in room	Choral Soc. Concert	Dance in Union	Coffee with friends
10–11	Listening to records	Coffee	Coffee	Coffee	Coffee	Listening to records	With friends
11–12	Work in room	With friends	With friends	With friends	Listening to records	Went to bed	With friends

Find the total hours for the week and then the average number for a day for each of the following activities: Sleep (average per day) 8; Meals and dressing ___; Class and laboratory 8 (1.1/7); Study 21 (3); Recreation and exercise ___ ; Student activities ___ ....

* Adapted from C. G. Wren and R. P. Larson (1955) *Studying Effectively* (2nd edn) Stanford University Press, p. 6.

Suggested reading

Client-centred, Rogerian counselling:
ROGERS, C. R. (1951) *Client-Centred Therapy* Boston, Mass.: Houghton, Mifflin Co.

Behaviour therapy:
WOLPE, J. (1969) *The Practice of Behaviour Therapy* Oxford: Pergamon Press.

Psychodrama:
MORENO, J. L. (1964) *Psychodrama* volume 1 (revised edn) New York: Beacon House.

Group work:
OHLSEN, M. M. (1970) *Group Counseling* New York: Holt, Rinehart & Winston.

Miscellaneous (on study skills):
WRENN, C. G. and LARSON, R. P. (1955) *Studying Effectively* (2nd edn) Stanford: Stanford University Press.

Publicity circular of the Keele Appointments and Counselling Service

The publicity circular takes the form of a four-page stiff-paper leaflet which can be retained for reference as a standing card on a student's mantelpiece or desk. Pages two, three and four are reproduced below together with an extract from page one.

PAGE ONE (extract)

The Appointments and Counselling Service offers assistance to those with educational, social, personal and emotional concerns. It is a professional and strictly confidential service.

Appointments to talk to a counsellor—which can be arranged very rapidly if necessary—may be booked by calling into our premises in Keele Hall and seeing the receptionist, or by telephoning.

PAGE TWO

What kind of service?

Counselling is relatively new in universities and it may be useful to give some idea of its place in this university . . .

'I'm having trouble deciding on my principal subjects.'

'Things are getting very bad at home. They're driving me up the wall and I don't know what to do.'

'I just don't seem able to make friends.'

'Can you tell me about openings in Market Research?'

'I just don't seem to be interested in my subjects any more. I can't concentrate.'

'I often wonder why I am at university—if only I could find some point in it all.'

'I thought it was about time I started to sort out my ideas about a career.'

'I wonder if you can tell me how to set about doing post-graduate research.'

'I often feel awful in discussion groups and tutorials. I wish I could do something about it.'

'I want to leave.'

'I'm sure I'm working too hard and getting nowhere.'

'The only boy-friend I ever had is packing me in and I can't work at all now.'

'I think I ought to see a psychiatrist.'

'I seem to be depressed all the time these days and I don't know why.'

PAGE THREE

Perhaps some of the above statements sound unlikely or even faintly comical. In fact, they illustrate the wide variety of questions and problems for which students have sought help in the past from the Appointments and Counselling Service. When some-one simply requires factual information, as is often the case, this is given in as straightforward a manner as possible and the inter-view may only last for a few minutes. On the other hand, where a student is experiencing more serious difficulties it is possible for him, if he so wishes, to maintain contact with a counsellor for longer periods of time, in which case counselling may well con-tinue over several interviews.

The counsellors do not attempt to impose their own values on those who seek their help. Instead they try to help a person see his own situation more clearly and then provide the oppor-tunity for exploring ways of developing more coping behaviour or of arriving at decisions.

In all cases whatever is said during an interview is confidential and will be revealed to no one without the student's permission. The counsellors are not members of the university teaching staff and reference in a counselling situation to academic departments or other officers of the University is only made with the express permission of the student concerned.

PAGE FOUR

Careers library and information service

Vocational counselling needs to be followed up by information seeking and perhaps work experience. To this end an up-to-date

Careers Library is maintained as an integral part of the Service. It is open to all members of the University during both term and vacation. The counsellors will also help students find those jobs or courses during the vacation which will be helpful to them vocationally. Details of many of these are available in the Careers Library, and our Administrative Assistant is usually available to answer informational enquiries of all kinds.

Vocational interest tests are available and many students, after consultation with a counsellor, have found these a valuable aid in exploring possible areas of employment. In addition frequent career discussions are held, with visiting speakers, and during the Spring Term a variety of employers come to the campus to see final year students or postgraduates who are interested in their organisations. Throughout the year a weekly Bulletin is published giving details of employment and post-graduate opportunities, and this is sent to all finalists and others who request it.

When are we open?

9 a.m. to 5 p.m. Monday to Friday (9 a.m. to 12 p.m. Saturdays, during term time only). In case of *urgency*, counsellors may be contacted at home.

Key texts

The books listed below are those which have perhaps done most to influence our thinking and practice. Nothing is included here for the sake of completeness or comprehensiveness. These are books which have communicated something to one or more of us at a level which has made it impossible to go on in quite the same way as before. Several of them have become well-thumbed reference books.

BLATNER, H. A. (1970) *Psychodrama, Rôle-playing and Action Methods, Theory and Practice* Published privately.

BLOCHER, D. H. (1966) *Developmental Counseling* New York: Ronald Press Co.

BOROW, H. (ed.) (1964) *Man in a World at Work* Boston, Mass.: Houghton, Mifflin Co.

ERIKSON, E. H. (1968) *Identity, Youth and Crisis* New York: W. W. Norton and Co.

JERSILD, A. T. (1955) *When Teachers Face Themselves* New York: Teachers College Press, Columbia University.

JOURARD, S. M. (1971) *The Transparent Self* (Revised edn) New York: Van Nostrand Reinhold Co.

MAY, R. (1970) *Love and Will* London: Souvenir Press.

MAYER-GROSS, W., SLATER, E. and ROTH, M. (1969) *Clinical Psychiatry* (3rd edn) London: Baillière, Tindall and Cassell.

OHLSEN, M. M. (1970) *Group Counseling* New York: Holt, Rinehart & Winston.

PAUK, W. (1962) *How to Study in College* Boston, Mass.: Houghton, Mifflin Co.

PERLS, F. S. (1969) *Gestalt Therapy Verbatim* Utah: Real People Press.

ROGERS, C. R. (1951) *Client-Centred Therapy* Boston, Mass.: Houghton, Mifflin Co.

ROGERS, C. R. (1961) *On Becoming a Person* London: Constable.

STORR, A. (1960) *The Integrity of the Personality* London: Heinemann.

SUPER, D. E. (1957) *The Psychology of Careers* New York: Harper and Row.

SUPER, D. E. and OVERSTREET, P. L. (1960) *The Vocational Maturity of Ninth-Grade Boys* New York: Teachers College Press, Columbia University.

TYLER, L. E. (1969) *The Work of the Counselor* (3rd edn) New York: Appleton-Century-Crofts.

WARNATH, C. F. (1971) *New Myths and Old Realities* San Francisco, California: Jossey-Bass Inc.

WOLPE, J. (1969) *The Practice of Behaviour Therapy* Oxford: Pergamon Press.

WRENN, C. G. (1962) *The Counselor in a Changing World* Washington, D.C.: American Personnel and Guidance Association.

YATES, A. J. (1970) *Behavior Therapy* New York: John Wiley and Sons Inc.

Index

abnormal psychology, 162
Abortion Act, 63, 118
academic difficulty, 29, 85-103 *passim*
  defined, 19, 85-6
  tables summarising, 22
  see also concentration, failure, study
    problems, subject choice
academic staff
  become counsellors, 159
  counsellor's relations with, 31-2,
    33, 34-6, 86, 91, 139
  courses in teaching for, 137
  difficulties facing, 143
  rôle in counselling, 102, 148
  selection of, 158
accommodation, students', *see* residence, halls of
Adams, J. F., 168
administration, university, 31-2, 37-8,
  39, 86, 132, 143
  scapegoat for complaints, 145-6
adolescents
  developmental needs of, 108, 150
  psychology of, 161-2
affective development, 9, 10, 146,
  153, 158
aggression, 132
Appointments Service, 16, 65
  officers of, 142, 154
aptitude tests, 76
assertive training, 170-1
Aston, University of, 154
audio-visual equipment, 161, 162

authority figures, 4, 33, 145-6
aversion therapy, 171
avoidance response, 95
auxiliary ego, 171, 172

behaviour
  counsellor's, 8, 60, 67, 81, 156, 162,
    165
  determined by custom, 108
  in group counselling, 173, 175
  influence on, 9, 13, 29, 90, 133, 179
  of staff, 28
  parents', 110-12, 146
  patterns, 6, 109, 115
  rehearsal, 172
  sexual, 118, 120
  social, 170, 173
  students', 75, 89, 92, 95, 116, 146,
    151, 170
  therapy, 55, 58, 96, 169-70, 171
  understanding of man's, 142, 160
behavioural engineers, 91-2, 101
breakdown, warnings of, 100, 113,
  148
British Student Health Association,
  149
Buber, Martin, 163

Camus, Albert, 163
careers, choosing of, *see* vocational
  guidance
Careers Advisers, misconception
  about, 69; *see also* counsellors

developmental psychology, 155
discipline, welfare officers and, 146-
147
drop-outs, university, 4, 89, 107, 109,
116, 138, 149, 151
drugs
and the law, 162
legal, 170
psycho-active, 149
use of, 63, 116, 128-31, 138

education
and mental health, 148
changing ideas on, 37
client's background, 49, 73
computers in, 152
conveyor-belt, 4-6, 107, 117
counselling, a part of, 3, 80-1, 108,
143, 153, 159, 160
learning skills, 87
university level, 141-2, 143
see also schools, teachers
educational psychology, 154
Education and Science, Department
of, 155
educators, counsellors as, 33, 87, 138,
160; *see also* teachers
embarrassment, elimination of, 72
emotional crises, 7, 29, 100, 111
in final year, 68, 81
interview during, 52-4
emotional development, 6, 9, 34
emotional disturbance, of students,
140
emotional relationships, 119-28, 131
breaking up of, 118, 123, 125-6
homosexual, 125-6
with tutors, 144
employers
expectations of, 142
practice interview for, 176
environment, effect on individual, 6,
153, 162
essay-writing difficulties, 87 93, 94,
99, 102

examinations
academic, 6, 85
fear of, 55-6, 87, 88, 91, 93, 94
stress during, 149, 164
therapeutic, 56
existence, search for meaning of, 4, 6,
117
existentialist philosophers, 163

failure, 107
academic, 86-9, 97-8, 100, 102
of counsellor to help, 92
false expectations of students
about careers, 71
about counsellors, 68-9
family history, 11, 49, 162
fantasy monologue, 172
fear, 6, 12, 13, 95, 169, 171, 177
counsellors', 104
of exams, 55-6, 87, 88, 91, 93, 94
of failure, 88, 97-8
of over-persuasion, 139
of parental disapproval, 109
of pregnancy, 115
of self-exploration, 68-9
of small groups, 35, 87, 95, 115, 170
feed-back, 87, 94, 178
femininity, 119; *see also* women, rôle
of
films, used in counsellor training, 161,
162
finance
dependence of students on help
with, 4, 50, 97
independence of school-leavers, 6
of universities, 145, 146
Freud, Sigmund, 11, 163
Freshers' groups, 174-5

Gay Liberation Front, 118
goals, establishment of new, 12, 13, 27
group counselling, 133, 163-4, 173-8;
see also psychodrama
*Group Process as a Helping Technique,
The* (Thompson and Kahn), 175